SAN FRANCISCO'S MUNICIPAL RAILWAY
MUNI

This Art Deco frieze adorns the entryway of the old Municipal Railway Headquarters at 949 Presidio Avenue. (San Francisco Municipal Railway Photographic Archive Collection.)

ON THE FRONT COVER: It is March 29, 1951, and the San Francisco Municipal Railway is in transition from an electric railway to a multimodal system operating modern streetcars, trolleys, and motor coaches as well as an ancient cable car fleet. Unused vestiges of its four tracks remain on San Francisco's main thoroughfare, Market Street, but only for a few more months. Muni's fleet includes the following, from right to left: 1948 forty-four-passenger Marmon-Herrington trolley coach 714 on the No. 6 line, 1939 "Magic Carpet" car 1002 on the L, 1923 "Iron Monster" 187 on the K, 1914 car 76 on the N, and 1949 Twin Coach 626 on the No. 21 line. Meanwhile, in the distance, a 1948 White bus turns onto Sutter Street. The pieces of equipment in this picture were the workhorses of Muni's fleet from 1914 through 1976. (San Francisco Municipal Railway Photographic Archive Collection X2681.)

ON THE BACK COVER: The Muni's logo was designed by city engineer M.M. O'Shaughnessy's staff and debuted on car sides around 1920 to replace costly letter board painting. The logo has been retired by successive image makeovers but still endures as the Muni's most recognizable brand. (San Francisco Municipal Railway Photographic Archive Collection M88.)

SAN FRANCISCO'S MUNICIPAL RAILWAY
MUNI

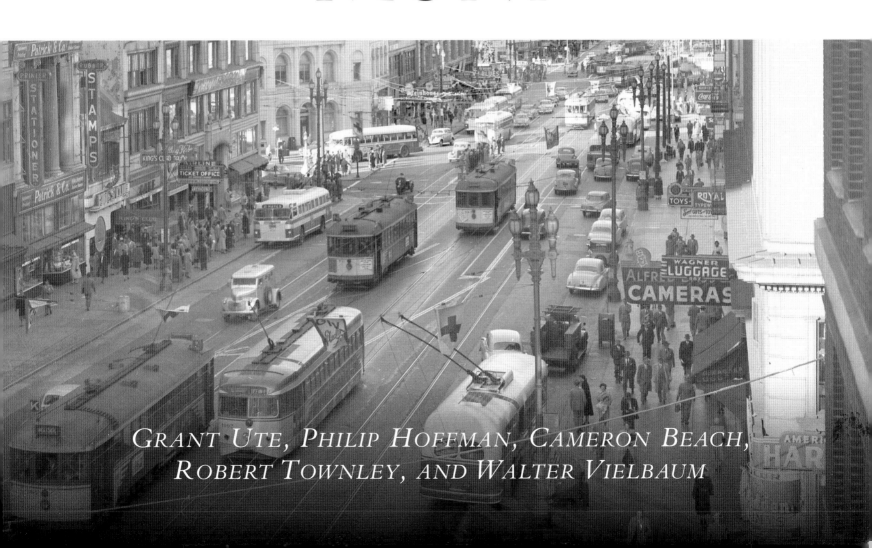

*GRANT UTE, PHILIP HOFFMAN, CAMERON BEACH,
ROBERT TOWNLEY, AND WALTER VIELBAUM*

Published by Arcadia Publishing
Charleston, South Carolina

Printed in the United States of America

Library of Congress Control Number: 2011925049

For all general information, please contact Arcadia Publishing:
Telephone 843-853-2070
Fax 843-853-0044
E-mail sales@arcadiapublishing.com
For customer service and orders:
Toll-Free 1-888-313-2665

Visit us on the Internet at www.arcadiapublishing.com

<u>IN MEMORIAM</u>

Authors Cameron Beach (January 26, 1949–March 18, 2011) and Philip Hoffman (November 10, 1930–April 20, 2011) Both saw this book project through to completion, but not into print. This book is a testament to their joyous enthusiasm for the city of San Francisco, its transit history, and particularly the Municipal Railway.

This book is dedicated to the Muni employees who worked long split-shifts on drafty platforms, toiled in dangerous sheave pits, fielded irate citizen complaints about the failings of a few peers, drove a car or bus or stood a traffic check alone in a dangerous neighborhood, and practiced the best skills of their trade, and to Muni's administrative staff who have been subject at times to political inquisitions, knowing that the truth would not be heeded. As the Muni celebrates its centennial, we recognize your dedication to taking us where our forefathers dreamed that we might go.

CONTENTS

ACKNOWLEDGMENTS

The authors wish to thank several people without whose assistance this book would not have been possible. First of all, under the direction of archivist Heather Moran and head photographer Carmen Magana, the Municipal Railway Photographic Department made this project possible by providing access to the agency's wonderful image collection. City archivist Susan Goldstein and San Francisco Public Library photograph curator Christina Moretta have assisted in locating images in the San Francisco History Center Collection. Allan Fisher and Charles Vercelli of the Bay Area Electric Railroad Association's Western Railway Museum Archive generously provided access to its extensive San Francisco Collection. Art Curtis, Angelo Figone, and Peter Straus provided their first-hand perspective on the railway's last 40 years. Finally, we appreciate the assistance of Harry Aitken, who made numerous valuable editorial suggestions.

Unless otherwise credited, the images in this volume appear courtesy of the Municipal Railway Photographic Archive (SFMR), San Francisco History Center of the San Francisco Public Library (SFPL), the Bay Area Electric Railroad Association Western Railway Museum Archive (BAERA), or the San Francisco Railway Archive (SFRA). Whenever possible, images are identified by photographer and collection number as follows: U (United Railroads); W or A (San Francisco Board of Works); D, M, T, or X (San Francisco Public Utilities Commission); or Y (San Francisco Municipal Railway). Kevin Sheridan provided many of the contemporary images of the F and T lines. His work can be seen in color at www.pbase.com/bythabay.

INTRODUCTION

When it clanged onto the scene in 1912, the San Francisco Municipal Railway was the first publicly owned transit system in a major American city. Today, it is the nation's seventh largest public transit system serving the heart of one of the country's largest metropolitan areas. It carries more passengers each day than the combined ridership of four other Bay Area carriers (Bay Area Rapid Transit District, Alameda-Contra Costa Transit District, SamTrans, and Caltrain). Two different Muni streetcar lines each board more riders a day than the entire Santa Clara Valley Transit Authority light rail system.

If San Franciscans have a love/hate relationship with the system they call "Muni," that is because they depend on it like almost no other city dwellers and desperately want it to be a success. Like any critical municipal service, when Muni works well, no one notices, but when it fails, everyone does. Every San Franciscan has a "Muni story."

During the first decade of the 20th century, San Francisco voters were asked four times to pass a bond issue to form a municipal transportation system. When the measure finally passed in December 1909, Mayor Edward Robeson Taylor gushed:

> This is great . . . The Geary Street road will now be built and run by the people and for the people. This marks an epoch. It means civic freedom . . . Some day our children's children will look back with wonder at the things we have stood for and suffered. Public utilities run . . . by the people . . . will give service to the public.

A century later, we owe it to these visionaries to look back on their venture. This is the story of how San Francisco's progressive civic experiment in a "people's railway" showed America how to use a municipal enterprise to expand and develop a frontier city, and it continues to show how streetcars can be a vehicle to revitalize a major urban center. While many today are tempted to find fault with government, maybe we "children's children" should wonder instead at our grandparents' belief in what a "government of better intentions" could accomplish. Hop on as we trace Muni's remarkable construction and development through the past 100 years and follow its growth into the most complex transit system in the country.

Transit franchises in San Francisco had been staked out with an eye to real estate development. Radial east-west lines anchored the population, transportation, retail and commercial centers. The city's public transit began as a competing tangle rather than a coherent system. With the formation of the Market Street Railway (MSRy) in 1893, a number of formerly competing franchises were amalgamated into one company, allowing transfers that afforded some degree of connection for a nickel basic fare. This over-leveraged property was sold off to a Baltimore investment syndicate in 1902 and renamed the United Railroads of San Francisco (URR.) Above, passengers stream toward the Ferry Building during the evening rush hour on August 23, 1905, while cable cars back up on Market Street waiting to use the double-tracked turntable. Meanwhile, a California Street horse car and a turning single-ended Sacramento-Clay cable car add to the action. (SFMR U551.)

OPPOSITE: On the morning of January 9, 1906, San Francisco gave no hint of disaster a few months away. In a time before the automobile, cable cars provided mobility for the masses on backbone routes on Market, Sutter, and Geary Streets. The private United Railroads controlled most transit services but was blocked from electrifying Market Street by a powerful city beautiful movement. Within 100 days, all that would change. Here, inbound Haight car 155 crosses Kearny and Third Streets at Market Street's "Newspaper Square," where the *San Francisco Examiner, Chronicle,* and *Call* newspapers were headquartered. (SFMR U657.)

ONE

PROGRESSIVE DREAM OF PUBLIC OWNERSHIP 1910–1912

At the dawn of the 20th century, San Francisco was the ninth largest city in America and the biggest one west of St. Louis. The city had become a rich financial center with links to vast mining interests. Largely self-sufficient industrially, it was also the site of tremendous technological change. While its elite capitalists, shippers, manufacturers, mining moguls, and suppliers had erected palatial mansions on high ground and enjoyed the fineries of great retail establishments and a sophisticated entertainment zone, the city's infrastructure was primitive. Located on a peninsula and divided by

a "spine" that separated its "outside lands" from its densely populated northeastern quadrant, its geography made hilltop neighborhoods inaccessible until the invention here of the cable car. In an era before the family automobile, street railways were the means to expand the city by opening new residential areas, and these railways returned millions on investments, a nickel at a time. San Francisco was, however, politically hobbled, having lost "home rule" due to political corruption. The reform politics of Progressivism infused its 1900 city charter with the vision of

public ownership of all utilities, including public transit. In this environment, though, everything had to be negotiated through an administration controlled by political boss Abraham Ruef. The Union Labor Party then in power delivered the votes for his machine. Despite manifest corruption, a reform slate was unable to oust them in 1905. "Handsome Gene" Schmitz, the former president of the Musician's Union, presided as mayor.

BURNING OF SAN FRANCISCO MORNING APRIL 18 '06

Early on April 18, 1906, a magnitude 8.4 earthquake shook San Francisco, and a subsequent three-day firestorm destroyed a third of the city, including its central business and residential districts. Thousands were killed or injured and hundreds of thousands displaced. This offered an opportunity to affect the Burnham Plan that in 1904 proposed a web of Parisian-style boulevards. Nonetheless, expediency prevented any major change to the problematic original grid work of streets laid out on steep hills. United Railroads photographer John Henry Mentz captured the scene at Alamo Square as stunned San Franciscans watched the "Ham and Eggs Fire" destroy Hayes Valley. (SFMR U822.)

The city hall was destroyed and much of the cable system was in shambles. URR photographer John Henry Mentz rushed from his Washington Street home and captured the earthquake damage to the Washington–Mason car house. Car 455 had been waiting to pull out when the earthquake toppled the powerhouse chimney. Later, a fire would rage through and destroy the building and all the cars. (Above, SFMR U831; below, SFMR U776A.)

Being the strategic gateway to America's newly acquired influence in the Pacific, with a relatively young resilient population, there was no doubt that San Francisco would be rebuilt. Nonetheless, the major part of San Francisco's public transit system had been destroyed, and its reestablishment was deemed an essential priority for recovery. (BAERA 17987.)

Within 10 days of the fire being extinguished, electric wires were strung, allowing the replacement of cable service on Market Street. This permitted San Francisco's 250,000 exiles to traverse the 500-city block moonscape that was the remains of the central business and residential districts to access the Potrero, Mission, and Western Addition Districts, where the commercial and entertainment industries relocated. Political boss Abraham Ruef administered massive amounts of "boodle" to lubricate the political authorization of trolley wires on Market Street to the Ferry Building. Mayor Eugene Schmitz, Ruef, and URR officials pose beside the private car *San Francisco* at the ferry on the opening day of electric streetcar service, May 3, 1906. (SFMR U835.)

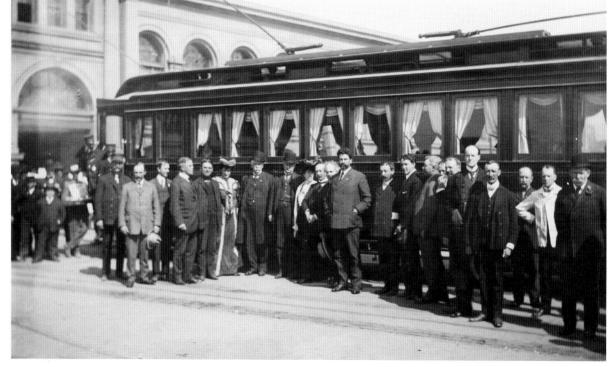

While the city hall was destroyed, the United States Mint on Fifth and Mission Streets and the post office at Seventh Street, shown here on May 12, 1906, survived. The URR poured in millions of dollars from Eastern investors and became one of the largest employers during San Francisco's reconstruction period. URR's photographer, John Henry Mentz, documented San Francisco's survival for out-of-town investors. Nonetheless, reconstruction projects languished, which resulted in at least two people drowning in URR construction zones south of Market. (SFMR U816.)

Staffing problems prevailed on the URR as crews found better wages in abundant reconstruction jobs. Dangerous overcrowding was commonplace due to irregular schedules. Safety was also compromised on inadequately maintained cars. Carmen worked under impossible conditions, and management refused to negotiate wage concessions. (Courtesy of John Hogan.)

On May 7, 1907, San Francisco's streetcar carmen went on strike when their contract ended. Violence, largely initiated by armed strikebreakers imported from the Eastern cities, resulted in over 30 deaths. It poisoned public opinion, fueled a boycott, and set the stage for decisive political action. Subsequently, the corruption involving trolley franchises was revealed, and sensationalized graft trials riveted and then exhausted the public. Prosecutorial zeal waned, especially when leading citizens began to be implicated. Above, the first strikebreaking car leaves the Turk and Fillmore barn on September 15, 1907. (California State Library Image 2481.)

THE CALL

VOLUME CVII—NO. 31.   SAN FRANCISCO, FRIDAY, DECEMBER 31, 1909.   PRICE FIVE CENTS.

31,185 For

Geary Street Bonds Win

11,694 Against

SMASHING VICTORY WON BY PEOPLE IN BATTLE FOR CITY OWNED ROAD

Protest Against Corporation Rule Voiced by Overwhelming Majority of Votes Cast for Municipal Street Railway

Given the mounting public perception of the role of the URR in civic ills, progressives proposed that the city operate a municipal railway for public benefit and profit. The opposition painted the "street railroad scheme" as a "white elephant" and cautioned against creating an immediate constituency of workers whose wage demands would be hard for politicians to refuse. The San Francisco *Call* countered with an editorial campaign, shown above, featuring its cartoonist John C. Terry painting URR officials and *Chronicle* publisher De Young as the villains. After four attempts, the Progressive dream of municipal management of street railways finally became a reality with the passage of the bond issue in a December 30, 1909, special election.

A GOOD BEGINNING FOR 1910

This cartoon reveals the *Call*'s optimism about the two municipal initiatives—the just passed municipal railway and the soon-to-be-voted-on Hetch Hetchy Water System bonds designed to address the water supply problem that also limited San Francisco's growth.

OPPOSITE: Mayor Taylor addresses a large audience at what may be the dedication of the original High School of Commerce at Grove and Larkin Streets. Note the dome of the Hall of Records in the background. Damaged in the earthquake, it was not removed for many years. (SFPL AAF0933.)

SAN FRANCISCO SHOWS HOW
1912–1914

The San Francisco Municipal Railway, "Muni," was a concept that needed to be built with efficiency and without corruption. In the San Francisco of 1910, that would be a tall order. After the board of supervisors was removed from office and Mayor Schmitz indicted, an unlikely candidate emerged as his replacement.

Eugene Robeson Taylor, a doctor, lawyer, and poet, was appointed and immediately acted decisively, firing corrupt officials and installing "a government of better intentions." He appointed Marsden Manson as city engineer. Manson was a civil engineer who had been one of the first State Highway commissioners and an advisor to

the State Harbor Commission and to the mayor immediately after the 1906 disaster. Manson and his staff designed the municipal railway and the Stockton Street Tunnel and outlined the shape of the Hetch Hetchy Water System.

At the Fifth Avenue and Fulton Street wye, cars, like former Haight Street car 167, were turned with the help of a tethered horse, shown above on May 3, 1912—two days before abandonment. (Photograph by F.T. Hill; BAERA 23184.)

The city's plan was to exercise its right to take over expiring franchises, build a modern electric railway with bond issues, operate it with its own employees, and use the profits to pay off the bonds. The Geary Street, Park & Ocean cable lines survived the 1906 cataclysm and operated surplus URR cars from Geary and Market Streets to Golden Gate Park. The inner terminal was San Francisco's busiest intersection, shown above in 1909, with former Valencia Street car 17 on the turntable in front of Charles De Young's Chronicle Building. Across the street, the reconstruction of the fire-damaged Palace Hotel is just finishing. After the fire, the line's outer terminal was cut back from Twelfth Avenue to Fifth Avenue and Fulton Street due to the discontinuance of the McAllister cable on Fulton Street. (BAERA 51183.)

Pavement Breaker – Geary St.

In 1912, with the Geary Street, Park & Ocean Railroad's operating permit expiring, the city began work in earnest, hiring day laborers to remove the cable system along the three-mile route. Note here that overhead trolley wire had already been strung before major track demolition and construction were started. This view looks east on Geary Street from Stockton Street on August 12, 1912. (SFMR W611.)

The staff of the board of works consisted of many young, competent graduates of the University of California. They designed and supervised construction of a reinforced concrete car house at Geary Street and Masonic Avenue. The board of works' photography department documented the construction of the line. The original one-story elevation of the Geary car house is shown above on August 7, 1913. The second-floor offices were added in 1915, as pictured below on April 12, 1923. (Above, BAERA W1546; below, SFMR 8636.)

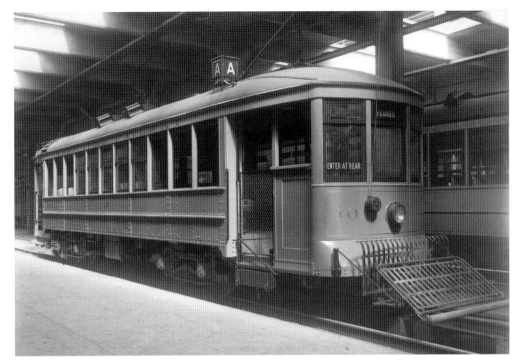

Many elements of the Geary Street line were suggested by nationally recognized transit consultant Bion J. Arnold. He designed the "Arnold" or "A-type" cars, such as new car 10, shown above on December 20, 1912, in the recently completed Geary car house. These cars were powerful and equipped with modern control and safety equipment, such as the Eclipse fender that functioned to prevent any pedestrians from falling beneath. They were designed with single seating on one side to speed loading. (Above, SFMR W1323; below, SFMR W1349.)

Thousands turned out for the formal opening of the line on December 28, 1912, when a total of 10 cars began service on the A Geary Street-Park line from Kearny Street to Tenth Avenue and Fulton Street via Geary Street and Tenth Avenue. At the opening, a single shuttle car served the B Geary Street line between Tenth and Thirty-third Avenues. (SFMR Collection.)

Shown above on February 1, 1912, Geary Street, Park & Ocean cable car 5 ran one of its last trips through the intersection of Geary and Jones Streets under already-strung trolley wire. At right, this unique photograph shows a packed car 1 underway in the same intersection as its inaugural trip on December 28, 1912, with a chase automobile in pursuit. As late as 1912, the reconstruction of downtown San Francisco was not complete. (Above, SFMR U3411; right, SFPL AAC8846.)

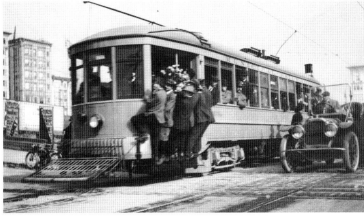

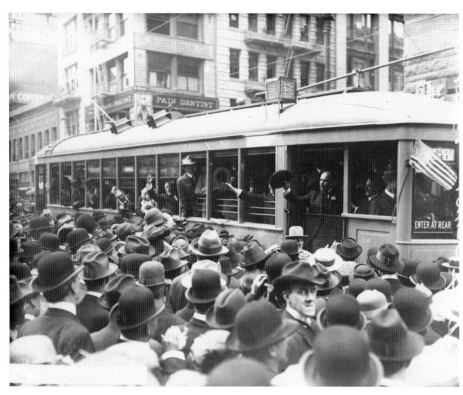

The city's next move was to extend the Geary Street line to the ferry. This could only be done after the expiration of the URR's subsidiary Sutter Street Railway franchise to operate on lower Market Street east of Sutter Street on a set of outside tracks. After defeating a legal challenge from the United Railroads, Muni gained access to the outer loop at the ferry through the Lower Market Street Compromise, where they paid for power and a fair share of maintenance costs of the URR trackage. The city then built outer tracks two blocks from Geary Street to Sutter Street to connect to existing URR tracks at Sutter. Mayor Rolph, above, addressed the crowd at Kearny Street before leaving on the first car to the ferry on June 25, 1913. That same day, the B Geary Street line was extended from Thirty-third Avenue to the beach via Thirty-third Avenue, Balboa Street, Forty-fifth Avenue, and Cabrillo Street to a crossover just west of Forty-ninth Avenue (now La Playa Street). In the San Francisco *Examiner* photograph pictured below, passengers board at Tenth Avenue and Geary Street for some of the first rides to the beach. (Above, BAERA 50707; below, SFRA Grant Ute Collection.)

In July 1916, a Muni D Van Ness car waits to enter Market Street as soon as the jitneys and outbound URR No. 7 car 117 get underway. Jitneys were private automobiles that offered rides for a nickel. By the time of this photograph, they were considered a threat to street railways, which had large capital costs and paid license fees. When the conductor signals "two bells" to indicate no traffic from behind, the motorman of the outbound B Geary will make the right turn onto Geary Street. (BAERA 4861 W3488.)

Despite the date on the tower, it is really the summer of 1914 and San Francisco seems ready to "Welcome the World" to the long-awaited Panama-Pacific International Exposition that would open February 22, 1915. The A car carries a ballpark sign indicating that its destination was Ewing Field on the newly constructed Masonic Avenue spur to Turk Street. Both the San Francisco Seals and the Oakland Oaks played home games there during the 1914 season. (SFPL AAD6272.)

OPPOSITE: The Tower of Jewels dominates the Panama-Pacific International Exposition's main gate at Scott and Chestnut Streets. Muni provided exclusive service to the main gate via four different routes. (SFRA Richard Schlaich Collection.)

THREE

THE CITY INVITES THE WORLD
1915

When San Francisco was chosen in 1911 to host the Panama-Pacific International Exposition, President Taft is reported to have said that it was selected because "San Francisco knows how." Planners recognized that an exposition without crowding would be a failure. The challenge was that under the existing franchise system, the private United Railroads had no incentive to invest capital in new lines. The burden of providing most of the public transportation for the visitors would fall on the fledgling municipal railway. This afforded the administration an opportunity to expand the Muni into the northern part of the city and potentially reap thousands of dollars in fares. The city took advantage of the expiration of the independent Presidio & Ferries Railroad franchise and took over its Union Street line and gave it the designation E. The rest of the lines to the exposition would have to be built by Muni. The task to do so fell to city engineer Maurice M. O'Shaughnessy, who replaced Manson in 1912 when James "Sunny Jim" Rolph became mayor.

The Presidio & Ferries Railroad was an independent company that operated two-car "dummy-and trailer" cable cars, shown at left on Union Street and west of Broderick Street around 1905. The earthquake totally destroyed the road, sustaining damage like this massive track dislocation on Union Street, west of Steiner Street. All of its rolling stock and its powerhouse at Leavenworth Street were destroyed in the subsequent fire. (Left, SFRA Richard Schlaich Collection; below, SFMR U1051.)

#1819 Union & Gough Sts. 9-25-08

During 1907, the Presidio & Ferries had contracted with the United Railroads to rebuild the line as an electric railway utilizing surplus URR single-truck dinkies, originally constructed in 1895. The United Railroads documented the work on September 25, 1908, and this photograph shows the switch at Union and Gough Streets leading to the car house on Filbert Street. When the franchise expired in early 1913, the city acquired the equipment and property and hired the staff, including the manager, who became the superintendent of the Muni's new Seventeenth Street (later Potrero) Division. (SFMR U1819.)

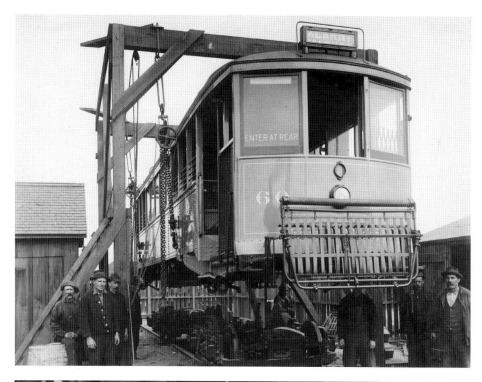

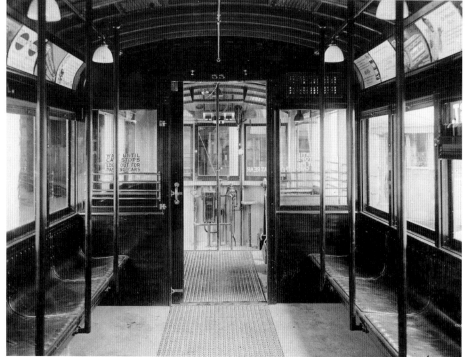

In addition to the construction of five lines on California Street, Van Ness Avenue, Stockton Street, Potrero Avenue, and Church Street, the 1913 bond issue also allowed for the addition of 125 cars of an improved design overseen by the new city engineer. The "B-type" cars were lighter and faster, loading with more platform room and wider aisles. Below, note the curtains on the center section windows of car 55. (Above, W1934, courtesy of Emiliano Echeverria; below, W1940 BAERA 45640.)

O'Shaughnessy's grey "Battleships" were actually a variant on a United Railroads 1913 car design—perhaps prompting this January 22, 1915, United Railroads photograph. These cars would prove to be the backbone of the Muni fleet for the next 44 years. Two cars (130 and 162) still operate in Muni's historic fleet. (SFMR U4760.)

One of Bion Arnold's ambitious suggestions was to link the exposition's grounds to downtown by way of North Beach and a tunnel on Stockton Street. A 1913 bond issue paid for the actual street railway line and equipment. The new wider cars, such as the one shown inbound on Stockton Street south of Vallejo in 1916, provided early service on the F Stockton line. Because Stockton Street was so narrow, the original "Arnold cars" soon found a home there. (SFMR W3769.)

The Stockton Tunnel, shown above around the beginning of 1915, linked previously isolated North Beach to the retail shopping district and Southern Pacific Depot, making Stockton Street a major crosstown artery. The board of works team designed this project with the tunnel financed by a special assessment district, a novel funding mechanism where the properties benefiting from an improvement paid additional taxes to cover its cost. When assistant superintendent Fred Boeken drove the first F line car (156) through the Stockton Tunnel on December 29, 1914, San Francisco still had blocks that had not been rebuilt. (SFMR W1916.)

When the Van Ness Avenue line opened on August 15, 1915, the framework of the dome of city hall was taking shape over the new Civic Center. The crowd at Van Ness Avenue and Market Street was intent upon Mayor Rolph's address from the back of special first car 64. An Irish setter lopes through the crowd. (Above, SFRA Richard Schlaich Collection; below, BAERA 50618.)

The opening of the line on Van Ness Avenue drew thousands. Note how the URR's Jackson cable car had to carefully negotiate its way through the throng. The H line terminated at a loop on Laguna Street, which gave Muni the closest connection to the "Fun Zone" at the east end of the exposition's grounds. The route also allowed for the creation of a D line that utilized the Geary Street route east of Van Ness Avenue and the E Union Street line west of Van Ness. It provided direct service from the ferry to the exposition's main gate. A car on the I line, which ran on weekends and holidays throughout the entire exposition, is seen below on Van Ness Avenue, south of Vallejo Street. It traveled from Thirty-third Avenue and Geary Street via Van Ness Avenue and the D line route exposition loop. (Above, BAERA 50619; below, California State Library, Hamilton Henry Dobbin Collection.)

Construction of the F line tracks on Columbus Avenue also allowed a direct connection from the ferry over a Columbus Avenue route, which was designated J before that letter was reassigned to the Church Street line later on. At left, original J cars pass on Columbus Street, south of Broadway Street. With the expiration of the URR California Street franchise, a new C line was constructed from the Geary Street trunk line at Second Avenue via Second Avenue, Cornwall Street, and California Street to Thirty-third Avenue. Given the United Railroads' reluctance to build any new lines, the city ensured adequate service to the exposition and positioned itself to reap thousands of dollars of earnings. (Photograph by J.B. Monaco; courtesy of SFPL.)

OPPOSITE: As can be seen by the Forward San Francisco sign behind him at the dedication ceremony on August 11, 1917, Mayor Rolph had decided to extend the Church Street line to the ferry. The "roar of the four" on Market Street began with a roar from the mayor who announced to the board of supervisors, just four days before, that he would "rule out of order" anyone who opposed the idea. The URR, embroiled in another major strike at the time, immediately requested an injunction the next day. Ultimately, the city's right to compete was upheld in the courts, and the shape of Market Street's character was formed for the next 32 years. (SFPL W4580.)

EXPANSION, THE STRATEGY FOR CIVIC GROWTH
1916–1931

The exposition was a success in no small measure due to Muni's providing efficient service to over 18 million visitors and workers, including 335,000 riders on closing day alone. At its end, however, one route, funded by the 1913 bond issue, had still not been built—the Church Street line. Originally scheduled to open in time for the exposition, it was planned to forge into United Railroads territory south of Market Street. The Church Street line presented geographic and political challenges. The URR saw the Church Street and the Twin Peaks Tunnel lines, then under construction, as a threat to its exclusive and lucrative Market Street franchise and refused Muni access to its tracks on Market Street to Geary Street. If Muni constructed outer tracks on Market Street as an alternative to using United Railroads', it would make URR cars less accessible. URR would fight this plan legally—all the way to the Supreme Court. But the city would prevail and use pioneer car lines as a way to open access to thousands of uninhabited acres west of Twin Peaks and, thus, add to its tax rolls. The din on Market Street became known as "the roar of the four (tracks)."

The URR did not oppose the Church Street line operating as a crosstown line. It proposed a transfer to its Market Street line and, in exchange, offered more direct use of its Sixteenth Street trackage for Muni pull-outs to the Church Street line from the new Seventeenth Street car house. Church Street's steep 19.3 percent grade from Twentieth to Twenty-first Streets posed a major engineering challenge. City engineer O'Shaughnessy proposed a cut through Mission Dolores Park and the residential area south of Twentieth Street, east of the summit of the hill. In this city engineer photograph, taken June 8, 1916, the Nineteenth Street Bridge has been constructed and tracks are in the park. Muni crews are laying the crossing of the URR's Eighteenth Street line. (SFMR W3826.)

The building of the Church Street line was not without organized community opposition. Homeowners, who bore the cost of the route through an assessment district, resisted the cost of the initial proposal to build a boulevard and pedestrian promenade. After nine proposals had been rejected, including a counterbalance trolley system similar to Fillmore Hill, a simple and slightly cheaper streetcar right-of-way was agreed upon. Work begins from Twentieth Street in January 1915 (above left). The URR kept a watchful eye on the progression of this work as demonstrated by this photograph of the same site (above right) in early May 1916. Built in an era before the term "NIMBY" had been coined, the route of the S curve, between Twentieth and Twenty-second Streets, literally was in people's backyards, as can be seen in the photograph at right. The area depicted in the image is located between Twenty-second and Church Streets and Twenty-first and Chattanooga Streets. (Above left, SFMR W2889; above right, BAERA 25222 U5346; right, SFMR W3255.)

On opening day, Mayor Rolph took the controls of car 72 and negotiated the Church Street grade through the multitude. (SFPL W4581.)

Since opening in 1916, the J line right-of-way through Dolores Park continues to be one of the most scenic trolley vistas in America. Here, car 104 climbs the grade between Nineteenth and Twentieth Streets on March 11, 1927. (BAERA 51536 W A110.)

FOREST HILL
IN 15 MINUTES

DEWEY BOULEVARD · 7TH AVENUE

Twin Peaks Tunnel

gives you a quick, comfortable way to reach your home in Forest Hill in the time it takes you to reach Fillmore Street now.

The concrete station with tiled roof shown in the circle above is the only subway station west of Twin Peaks. It will cost a quarter of a million dollars, and is included in the tunnel contract, so that it must be finished when the tunnel is finished.

The next rainy morning when you stand on a windy corner waiting for a street car which, as you step aboard, deftly empties a half-pint of water down your shivering spine, remember the cozy, warm, spacious waiting-room in Forest Hill Station, where you will be able to take your train in comfort.

Did you ever get a teaspoonful of water down your back? Don't it make you sore?

Forest Hill Station is a 5-minutes' walk from any part of Forest Hill—15 minutes downtown. See us soon.

We have some wonderful bargains in this beautiful home park.

Newell-Murdoch Co.
30 MONTGOMERY STREET

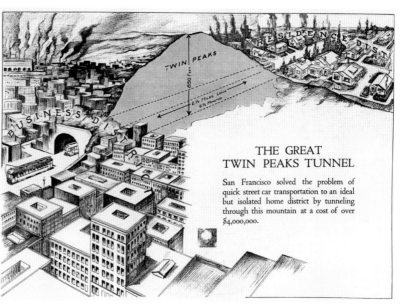

THE GREAT TWIN PEAKS TUNNEL

San Francisco solved the problem of quick street car transportation to an ideal but isolated home district by tunneling through this mountain at a cost of over $4,000,000.

The financing of the Twin Peaks Tunnel was paid for by another assessment district. Property owners of the nearly 5,000 acres west of Twin Peaks bore 75 percent of the cost with the final 25 percent paid by property owners in an area along the route east of Twin Peaks. Promoters jumped on the opportunity to advertise real estate developments, such as these advertisements touting the benefits of the soon-to-be-built Laguna Honda Station that served Forest Hill. (Both, SFRA Collection.)

Both the eastern and western portals were constructed using a "cut-and-cover" method for the first several hundred feet. On March 2, 1915, a steam shovel, shown above, loads a mule-drawn wagon—one shovel per wagon—at the western end of the tunnel. By April 8, work had progressed to laying the foundation and side forms, pictured below. (Above, BAERA 161 W2263; below, BAERA 163 W2326.)

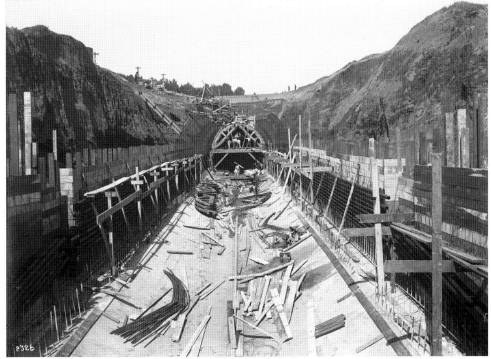

Tunneling was done by hand at this point in construction with wooden lagging and finished in concrete, as shown in this June 28, 1915, photograph. Crews hit rock and ground water while digging deeper in, but excavation continued on schedule. (BAERA 160 W2446.)

The classic West Portal facade was being finished in this January 1917 photograph. Temporary narrow-gauge tracks were used for the removal of soil. (SFMR W4017.)

This November 22, 1915, image of the West Portal area shows that the project was a "tunnel to nowhere." The tree line above the tunnel is probably located on Magellan (then De Soto) Street or Dorantes Avenue. The Claremont Station sign refers to the name of the land development to the east of what is now Claremont Boulevard and above Ulloa Street. All during the construction, it was unclear what railway lines would use the tunnel and the West Portal Station, as it came to be called. Chief engineer O'Shaughnessy was amenable to negotiating its use by the URR's Parkside, Twentieth Avenue, and Sloat Boulevard routes. (BAERA 164 W2849.)

In the only authorized use of the Twin Peaks Tunnel by private automobiles on June 15, 1917, an auto inspection tour was arranged for officials. Mitchell and Saxon automobiles left downtown on an "over-and-under" Twin Peaks tour, traversing the new Twin Peaks Boulevard to West Portal. (Both, photographs by Arthur Spaulding, SFMR Collection.)

After celebrations and photographs with an automobile advertising photographer, the cars entered the tunnel for what must have been a bone-jarring ride down hill over ties and ballast. Given the state of mufflers and emission control in those days, the trip to Castro Street, pictured below, must have been literally exhausting. Compare the condition of the whitewall tires upon exiting from the tunnel to the view on Twin Peaks Boulevard. On the occasion of the tunnel dedication on July 14, 1917, pedestrians were allowed to walk the 12,000 feet up hill from Castro to West Portal. (Both, photographs by Arthur Spaulding, SFMR Collection.)

When Mayor Rolph piloted car 117 out of the tunnel into the light at West Portal on February 3, 1918, police were on hand to control spectators. Note the switch for the proposed Taraval Street line. The special car continued on West Portal Avenue four more blocks to the end of the line at St. Francis Circle. Upon opening, K Market Street cars ran out of Muni's Geary Division from Bush Street and Van Ness Avenue to St. Francis Circle, over Van Ness Avenue and Market Street, via Twin Peaks Tunnel and West Portal Avenue. (SFMR M494.)

Absent any agreement with United Railroads at this time, the Muni nationally pioneered the operation of feeder buses to a street railway line. Two routes were laid out; one anticipated the eventual L Taraval Street line and served the Parkside District over Sloat Boulevard, Nineteenth Avenue, and Taraval Street to Thirty-third Avenue. The other, serving Westwood Park, another development benefiting from the tunnel, continued over what was to become the K Ingleside on Junipero Serra Boulevard and Ocean Avenue to Harold Street. (SFMR W5125.)

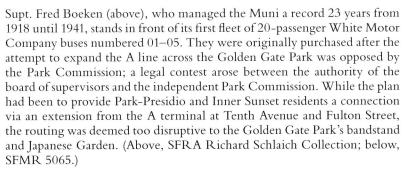

Supt. Fred Boeken (above), who managed the Muni a record 23 years from 1918 until 1941, stands in front of its first fleet of 20-passenger White Motor Company buses numbered 01–05. They were originally purchased after the attempt to expand the A line across the Golden Gate Park was opposed by the Park Commission; a legal contest arose between the authority of the board of supervisors and the independent Park Commission. While the plan had been to provide Park-Presidio and Inner Sunset residents a connection via an extension from the A terminal at Tenth Avenue and Fulton Street, the routing was deemed too disruptive to the Golden Gate Park's bandstand and Japanese Garden. (Above, SFRA Richard Schlaich Collection; below, SFMR 5065.)

Alternative crossing points were not as feasible, and as a compromise, the Muni No. 1 bus route (left) ran from Tenth Avenue and Fulton Street to Twenty-fifth and Irving Streets. Above, women board Muni coach 04 around 1918. (SFPL AAC7751.)

Aside from the United Railroads' concerns about losing its exclusive hold on the profitable Market Street traffic, the opposition claimed that four tracks on Market Street would create a dangerous barrier to pedestrians crossing the street to patronize retail stores, such as the Emporium on the south side. This February 14, 1917, city engineer photograph above shows a No. 17 Haight-Ingleside car at Market and Powell Streets. This route was one of the longest in the city—running from the ferry via Haight Street, Lincoln (then H) Street, Twentieth Avenue, Wawona Street, Nineteenth Avenue, Sloat Boulevard, and Ocean Avenue to Miramar Avenue in the Ingleside. Within two years, Muni's own K Market Street Tunnel line would cut this running time drastically. The result was that the No. 17 was diverted west on Sloat Boulevard to the beach. The effects of the addition of the outer tracks can be seen in the image below of construction looking east from Fourth and Market Streets on May 23, 1918. The clearance between cars was a mere 22 inches. (Above, BAERA 4862 W4058; below, SFMR Collection.)

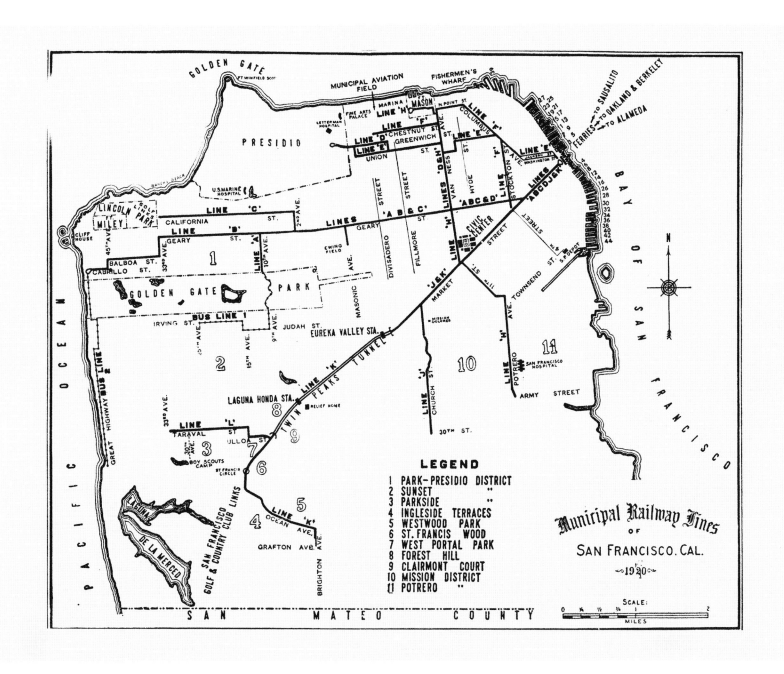

A May 1, 1920, public timetable map showed the extent of Muni's route system. The H Potrero was a "paper route," hauling many passengers on transfers as it bridged between the Market, Geary, and North Beach Streets routes. The pioneering bus routes at the beach and across Golden Gate Park show Muni's efforts to respond to service needs in these isolated areas. (BAERA 47198.)

By the early 1920s, automobile competition was affecting ridership, accident rates, and schedules. This 1921 photograph demonstrates "don'ts" for new drivers through an image of a woman almost being "clipped" by an eight-cylinder King as she boards a Van Ness Avenue car stopped at Vallejo Street, just ahead of an 1895 Union Street dinky. When Muni was founded, there were no traffic signals in all of San Francisco. By 1915, the first "traffic indicator" had been installed at the city's busiest intersection, Kearny and Market Streets, shown below in 1923. A traffic officer on a stand manually controlled the indicator. (Left, BAERA 50628; below, SFMR M455.)

O'Shaughnessy and the URR continued negotiating to arrange services west of Twin Peaks. While Muni controlled the Twin Peaks Tunnel, the URR had existing services to the Parkside District via its Parkside shuttle service on Twentieth Avenue, Taraval Street, and Thirty-third Avenue; No. 17 Haight-Ocean line on Twentieth Avenue, Wawona Street, Nineteenth Avenue, and Sloat Boulevard; and its No. 12 Ocean Avenue-Sloat Boulevard line. Ultimately, a compromise was worked out in the Ingleside where for a one-time cash payment and an operating expense agreement, the URR allowed the Muni K to traverse its No. 12 line tracks on Ocean Avenue as far as Miramar Avenue while Muni built an extension south from Ocean Avenue on Brighton to Grafton Avenues. The URR relinquished the Parkside line from Twentieth Avenue and Taraval Street to Thirty-third Avenue. Muni built a connection from West Portal Avenue and Ulloa Street to connect at Twentieth Avenue and Taraval Street and then rebuilt the URR Parkside shuttle tracks to Thirty-third Avenue. Just after this August 10, 1922, photograph, the Taraval Street line was extended from Thirty-third Avenue, shown above, to Forty-eight Avenue and Taraval Street. At the Forty-eight Avenue and Taraval Street terminal, shown below, one of the new O'Shaughnessy-designed J-type center entrance cars waits for no one in the middle of nowhere. Muni was making large expanses of real estate accessible, trading revenue losses for long-term expansion of the tax roles. Note the real estate office in the photograph above as well as the URR tracks turning south on Thirty-third Avenue. (Above, SFRA Richard Schlaich Collection; below, BAERA 50633.)

Muni was under almost constant political pressure to develop new car lines or bus feeder routes to serve San Francisco's expanding population, which had increased over 50 percent from 416,912 in 1910 to 634,394 in 1930. In December 1925, the Westwood Park Association gave the city three buses to extend the Muni No. 1 Park bus route southward from Forest Hill Station, shown on December 15, 1926, to the end of the MSRy No. 10 line at Gennessee Street and Monterey Boulevard. Seen below on March 11, 1927, one of the new buses enters St. Francis Wood from Monterey Boulevard onto Plymouth Avenue on its way to Golden Gate Park. (Above, SFMR W10621; below, BAERA 47219.)

On January 15, 1918, Muni instituted its crosstown bus route No. 2 from the end of the B Geary Street line at Cabrillo and the Great Highway to the end of the L Taraval Street line and south to Sloat Boulevard. On March 20, 1927, the Chutes at the beach can be seen in the background at the B line terminal. (SFMR A102.)

Due to low patronage and limited capacity, bus routes were generally money losers, and Muni struggled with them, considering at one point discontinuing free transfers. Instead, Muni management eventually saw them as a public benefit. The Embarcadero bus service began on January 27, 1927, with a sizeable subsidy by the State Port of San Francisco. Coach 017 is shown in front of Pier 5 where the SS *Harvard* is in port readying for its overnight voyage to Los Angeles. (BAERA 47217.)

In 1923, as pressure mounted to deliver services to the Inner Sunset and Cole Valley Districts, the city constructed a Sunset Tunnel, designed by O'Shaughnessy's staff. Originally planned to connect at Eureka Station, the tunnel was built eventually on an extension of Duboce Avenue. This 4,232-foot bore used improved construction techniques, including a moveable form, power shovel, and dump trucks, as shown in this image. Compare these methods to the means used in the Twin Peaks Tunnel shown on pages 43–44. (BAERA 4882 A352.)

By the time the Sunset Tunnel was dedicated on October 21, 1928, Mayor Rolph was an experienced motorman. Here, he runs the first N Judah car (102) through the Sunset Tunnel's West Portal. (BAERA 50638 A1493.)

A parade of cars carried civic officials to the Judah Street line dedication ceremony attended by thousands at Ocean Beach. (BAERA 51533 A1498.)

Relishing the moment and carrying the gate handle, the mayor donned his motorman's hat (complete with his union buttons) for the event. Sunny Jim was always one to recognize the extraordinary accomplishments of "Chief" M.M. O'Shaughnessy, shown with him on the dais at the beach at the dedication ceremony. At this time, the mayor aspired to the governor's office. Changes were also afoot to rewrite the San Francisco Charter to limit the power of the city engineer, who at one time earned a salary equal to that of the mayor, city attorney, and police chief combined. A new era lay ahead for Muni. (Above, BAERA 50641; below, SFMR A1500.)

In the early 1920s, United Railroads had been reorganized as the Market Street Railway, which later contracted a utilities management firm, the Byllesby Company, to operate its system. Under the direction of Samuel Kahn, it improved its performance and public image by constructing 250 cars in its own San Francisco shops, with such appointments as soundproofed flooring, cushioned seats, and a modern paint scheme. A Geary car has a chance opening to enter Market Street between two freshly painted Market Street Railway Balboa Street line cars sporting the new "zip stripe'" livery. Note that the Palace Hotel in the center of the photograph still had its original balconies. (SFMR D4279.)

OPPOSITE: Nosing its way between Market Street Railway's "White Front" cars onto Market Street from Geary Street, a Muni B adds to the "roar of the four." (BAERA 51186.)

DEPRESSION AND WAR
1932–1944

Prevented from purchasing its private competitor in the 1920s due to cost of the residual value of the franchises, the city also missed the opportunity to consolidate with their expiration in 1929. Muni finances were weighed down with politically popular, but financially unsuccessful, bus routes and the yet-to-be profitable pioneering L Taraval Street, M Oceanview, and N Judah Street lines. By 1930, the Market Street Railway had restored public confidence and an initiative passed by a considerable majority, allowing it a generous 25-year operating permit extension. The year 1932 also saw Sunny Jim Rolph inaugurated as governor and chief engineer O'Shaughnessy ushered aside through the new charter that took effect in January. The San Francisco Municipal Railway was essentially built, and San Francisco had an infrastructure that was modern and well constructed. Soon power and water revenues were starting to flow in from the Hetch Hetchy and water department enterprises. Angelo Rossi entered the mayor's office, and an independently appointed Public Utilities Commission oversaw the municipal enterprises of the Water Department, Hetch Hetchy project, the airport, and the bureau of street lighting. With this, Muni entered a new economic environment and an era of competition under new governance.

TAXE$ AND
THE
MUNICIPAL
RAILWAY
THE TRUTH
IN
BLACK AND WHITE

PUBLIC UTILITIES
COMMISSION

To address public confidence in Muni, during 1931 the city supervisors called in the State Railroad Commission to do a top-to-bottom analysis of the railway. The final report was generally favorable in terms of performance, safety, maintenance, morale, and lean administrative costs. However, it pointed out the relatively high costs for operating and maintenance personnel and some looming replacement expenditures. These included worn track along the busy Geary corridor, which had a car scheduled every 45 seconds during peak hours. The new San Francisco Public Utilities Commission responded with a public information campaign of its own. It was clear, though, that the days of operating profits were over. A *Call* photograph (above left), taken August 29, 1932, shows helpful conductor Will Hage assisting passenger Viletta Willison. About 22 years later in his career, Hage was recognized as "Muni Man of the Month" in September 1954. (Above left, SFPL AAC8721; below left, SFMR X3500; above, BAERA 47199.)

The inefficiency of three lines running on only four tracks on outer Market Street can clearly be seen in this August 19, 1935, view of Market Street at Castro Street. Here, the center tracks of the Market Street Railway No. 8 line swing left down Castro Street, while a Muni K car on the outer tracks, which were shared with the L, prepares to enter Twin Peaks Tunnel on its way to the Ingleside. Other than the addition of many homes in Twin Peaks in the background, this scene remained pretty much the same for another 38 years until the construction of the Muni Metro Station. Compare this scene to that in the photograph on page 115. (SFMR A4596.)

Muni finally found funds to address its worn out track from President Roosevelt's Works Progress Administration (WPA). This photograph documented the recently completed WPA rerailing of Union Street. There is plenty of parking available on Friday afternoon, September 25, 1936, on Union Street, east of Webster Street, in front of the Metropolitan Meats, Metropolitan Bakery, Metropolitan (later Metro) Theater, and the New Metro Beauty Shoppe. That is a 1932 Pierce-Arrow on the far left. (SFMR W A4910.)

In 1937, Muni was also able to use WPA funds to extend its L Taraval Street line down Forty-sixth Avenue (above) at Vicente Street on the way to the zoo and Fleishhacker Pool in direct competition to the Market Street Railway's No. 12 line. On April 8, 1940, rerailing work is under way on Geary Street at Mason Street. (Above, photograph by Will Whittaker, courtesy of Walter Vielbaum; below, BAERA 51717.)

Between casually parked cars on Baker Street, the E car above discharges a lone passenger at Greenwich Street before reuniting with the D on the way to the Presidio. This J-type car also ran on the H Potrero owl, which covered Chestnut Street; the short-lived 1932 O line rerouting on Union Street to Van Ness Avenue; as trippers on the F Stockton; and, for a time, on the L Taraval shuttle. The unique center-door "dinkies" were designed by the city engineer's staff to replace the 1895-era Union Street cars acquired from the Presidio & Ferries. Below, note the metal O'Shaughnessy-designed Muni logo in the roof arch. The E connected the Presidio to the ferry via Russian Hill, North Beach, and Washington or Jackson Streets through the crowded produce market area in what is now the Golden Gateway. (Above, photograph by Waldemar Sievers, courtesy of John Harder; below, SFMR D4738A.)

REMOVE THE STUMBLING BLOCK
then Modernize!

Once the Market Street Railway belongs to the people of San Francisco we will be free to rebuild, unify and modernize our transportation system.

The Public Utilities Commission has proposed a $11,978,000 rehabilitation program making the entire maximum cost of the project, $24,478,000. Favorable action on application for PWA funds will bring the total cost to below $20,000,000.

Under the proposed rehabilitation program one hundred and fifty modern, streamlined, noiseless cars and 108 trolley coaches would replace the back numbers now in use.

Other improvements would include reconstruction of tracks and extensions, and automotive coaches.

Own Your Own System – On a 5 Cent Fare

San Francisco has prospered and grown with its municipally owned transportation system.

The Municipal Railways have turned sand dunes into residential districts and have operated at a profit to taxpayers.

Municipal ownership has maintained the five cent fare for municipal railway riders . . .

THE GROWTH OF SAN FRANCISCO IS AT STAKE

LET'S MARCH AHEAD WITH THE FIVE CENT FARE!

Let's Build a Real 20th Century Metropolis with a unified transportation system owned by the people of San Francisco.

Vote for the Passage of Market Street Railway Purchase and Rehabilitation Bond Issue.

VOTE YES ON NUMBER 8

CENTRAL COMMITTEE FOR MODERN TRANSIT
S. W. Douglas, Chairman
George H. Allen, Secretary
325 MARSHALL SQUARE BUILDING   MARKET 8331

Here's A Business Proposition:

The Interior of a New Streamlined Street Car

WHY GIVE AWAY $7,000,000 a year
In Seven-Cent Fares to a Private Company?

When You Can **OWN** The Car System

AND ENJOY A 5-CENT FARE!
Universal Transfers, Unified Modern Transit, Safe Two-Man Cars

VOTE YES ON PROPOSITION NUMBER 8

Special Election, September 27, 1938

Despite the Market Street Railway gaining an extended permit in 1930, competition continued via the ballot box throughout the Depression. Under financial stress in 1935, it introduced one-man cars on all secondary routes. The city countered by sponsoring a two-man staffing ordinance. Additionally, the city allowed jitneys to compete only on Market Street Railway arteries. Ultimately, the company raised fares to 7¢—which was not lost on proponents of the unsuccessful September 1938 ballot measure to buy out the private competitor. The 2¢ fare hike was challenged, and proceeds were ordered into a trust fund pending resolution. (BAERA 47245.)

When rail service opened on the San Francisco-Oakland Bay Bridge, the Key System, Interurban Electric Railway, and Sacramento Northern Railway provided service to Oakland, Alameda, Contra Costa County, Sacramento, and as far away as Chico. This changed transit patterns in San Francisco overnight. The 1948 view of the streetcar ramps shows the three streetcar tracks as well as the Key System bus loading area under the awnings. (SFMR X1403.)

With diminishing ferry traffic, every other streetcar was diverted via First Street to the new bridge terminal. This image shows the massive traffic jam that ensued on January 16, 1939, when inside track cars had to cut in front of Muni cars on the outside tracks. This was ameliorated to some extent by assigning different lines to the ferry and bridge terminals. Weeks later, the Golden Gate International Exposition opened for a two-year run and demand returned for service back to the ferry. In anticipation of this, in late 1938, the E was moved from Potrero barn to Geary Street to rejoin the F. In a reprise of the original J Panama-Pacific International Exposition route, every third F operated over the east end of the E to the ferry. (SFMR Collection.)

Opened in 1925 to satisfy the property owners of the vast tracts in the Oceanview who had been paying for the Twin Peaks Assessment without receiving service, the M Oceanview line never covered its costs. A two-car shuttle ran from St. Francis Circle to Broad Street and Plymouth Avenue. Between 1939 and 1944, this was replaced with bus service. Above, Arnold car 43 discharges its passengers at St. Francis Circle. This March 29, 1926, view below looks south at the two-way intersection of Nineteenth Avenue and Junipero Serra Boulevard, which was protected only by a wigwag railroad signal. The vista shows the area as it appeared until Park Merced and San Francisco State College were built to the right and behind the photographer. (Above, photograph by John Gerrard Graham, SFPL AAX0210; below, SFMR W10256.)

As if to follow up on the pledge of the unsuccessful 1938 bond campaign, Muni purchased five streamlined cars to compete with the modernization program of the Market Street Railway. Completely enclosed, adorned with a deep blue and yellow paint scheme, well lit, and with a ride so smooth that Muni nicknamed them "Magic Carpet cars," they created a sensation when put on public display in November 1939. Car 1002 is shown at Stockton and Market Streets. It caused a roadblock at the choke-point terminal of the F Stockton. For the next decade, the 1002 and her four sisters would call the L Taraval home. (SFMR D4141B.)

With the expiration of the franchise on Howard Street, Muni continued its policy of assuming competing routes. Meanwhile, it also followed up on a recommendation of the 1931 State Railroad Commission report by venturing into the use of electric trolley buses. The Market Street Railway had introduced trolley coaches into San Francisco in 1935 when it converted its No. 33 Eighteenth Street–Park line. New St. Louis Car Company–built coach 509 lays over at the Beale Street inner terminal of the new R line that ran to Army and Howard Streets (as Caesar Chavez and South Van Ness Avenues were then called). Muni ACF Brill bus 063 provided a shuttle link to the Ferry Building. (SFMR A7022.)

Signs for the Crystal Palace Market, Embassy and United Artists theaters, the Flying A gas station, the bird cage signal, and the graphics on the wall featuring "Awful Fresh MacFarlane" candy are all long-gone features at Eighth and Market Streets. Happily, the Orpheum Theater and two streetcars (like the J in this picture) still survive. (Photograph by Waldemar Sievers; courtesy of John Harder.)

WOMEN WANTED
TO MAN THIS CAR: CREW OFF TO WAR!

START TODAY AT FULL PAY
As Motorman or Conductor

TRAIN AT OUR EXPENSE FOR CIVIL SERVICE POSITIONS WITH MUNICIPAL RAILWAY. GOOD FOR THE DURATION AND SIX MONTHS THEREAFTER.

NO EXPERIENCE REQUIRED!

Beginning the moment you start training at our expense, this will be your wage range:

First six months........ 85c per hour
Second six months.......87½c per hour
Third six months........ 90c per hour
Thereafter ....92½c per hour

Time and one-half for all overtime worked. Pension, sick leave and vacation rights, as earned, under Charter provisions. Work in a handsome, official uniform under full Civil Service security close to your home and contribute your share to the war effort by getting war plant employes to their jobs.

ALSO OPEN TO MEN!

APPLY AT ONCE
ROOM 151, CITY HALL

With crews off to war (or more lucrative shipyard jobs), both the Muni and Market Street Railway hired female crews. Women Muni employees were hired "for the duration and six months," whereas Market Street hired them as permanent employees. When the war ended, only the former Market Street female employees had permanent positions. Here, "motorette" Dolores Piluso (left) and "conductorette" Ellen Peterson (center) model the stylish uniforms. Ellen was not actually a Muni employee, but rather a water department worker invited to pose as a model. (Left, SFMR D4356D; center, BAERA 32176; right, SFMR 4756A.)

On its 30th anniversary on December 28, 1942, two of Muni's original 1912 platform men, conductor Mark Moorhard and motorman Louis Litzius, pose beside car 1 at the Geary car house. All three are members of the "million-mile club." Little did anyone know that car 1 would be drafted for more than the duration of the war and be completely rebuilt to star in Muni's centennial 70 years later. (SFRA Richard Schlaich Collection.)

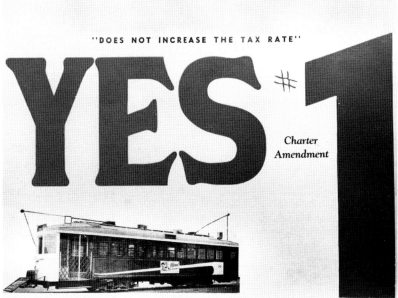

"DOES NOT INCREASE THE TAX RATE"

YES #1

Charter Amendment

ENDORSED BY ALL CIVIC AND IMPROVEMENT CLUBS

TO OUR CITIZENS:

After serving You over a half century = Thank you & goodbye

MARKET STREET RAILWAY COMPANY
SAMUEL KAHN, President

While the Market Street Railway soldiered on during World War II, its physical plant and rolling stock were completely worn out. A $7.5-million bond issue to purchase the property finally passed on May 16, 1944. It specified that the bonds were to be paid for out of Muni wartime profits and earnings of the Market Street Railway. Muni acquired 439 streetcars, 39 cable cars, 139 motor coaches, 9 trolley coaches, and 30 work cars along with 41 lines and all carbarns, shops, right-of-ways, and substations. The Market Street Railway could trace its corporate lineage back to 1892, and this window sign bids adieu to its riders. (Left, Robert Townley; above, Walter Vielbaum.)

Roger Lapham ran for mayor in 1943 on a platform calling for the purchase of the Market Street Railway. At 5:00 a.m. on September 29, 1944, he achieved his goal and was ceremonial motorman with the first pull out of this former Market Street Railway No. 31 Balboa car. With universal transfer privileges over all lines, San Francisco was the last major city to abandon the nickel fare. (SFMR Collection.)

OPPOSITE: Fares was raised to 7¢ with the merger, and the Muni's Oscar Larsen painted out the 5¢ fare for this newspaper shot. (SFPL AAC8412.)

MERGER, CONVERSION, AND THE STRUGGLES OF UNIFICATION 1944–1952

With unification, Muni faced immediate and longer-term challenges. First, employees had to be brought into civil service—raising issues since some Market Street employees were not US citizens. The merger of seniority lists provoked opposition from the Municipal Carmen's Union, considering many former Market employees had been employed before Muni came into existence in 1912. Operations had to be amalgamated, and the staffs of the formerly rival organizations had to be unified as members of a common enterprise. With the war's end, many workers returned to their jobs to find that much of the former Market Street system had to be rebuilt. This afforded management the opportunity to employ more economical gas and electric buses. With all this on the agenda, the competing systems were largely rebuilt, sometimes only changing mode from streetcar to electric trolley or motor coach. Due to the urgency of the task, many of the through-routing ideas of O'Shaughnessy's 1929 amalgamation plan were not followed.

The Market Street Railway employees were its primary assets. The workforce was larger than Muni's and contained many skilled craftspeople and long-term employees, including Nick Kruer (lower left), who became the second highest in seniority at Muni. At the merger, Market employees enjoyed a pay raise and eligibility for pension and social security benefits. As this May 22, 1947, photograph of Sutro car house employees shows, the workforce of postwar Muni was quite diverse. African American men and women had found new careers through wartime work opportunities. (SFMR X1266.)

After consolidation, there were numerous training needs. New crews had to be oriented, and about 80 percent of seasoned motormen and conductors had to be retrained to operate trolley or motor coaches. On February 26, 1947, a motorman gets hands-on training at McAllister barn's mock-up, which demonstrated all the elements of a two-man streetcar. Accident prevention training emphasized safety as more and more automobiles crowded the streets with the end of gas and tire rationing. (SFMR X1199.)

Through 1948, Muni was in transition with old Market Street Railway equipment, such as No. 22 Fillmore California Comfort Car 906, No. 24 line Yellow Coach 165, and Washington and Jackson cable car 526, all repainted into Muni's postwar green and cream livery. Three types of vehicles were posed at Fillmore and Jackson Streets in front of the Calvary Presbyterian Church. Of the vehicles, only car 526 survives on the Powell Street lines today. (SFMR X1771.)

Generally, lines retained their position on inside or outside tracks on Market Street, but this changed as the outer tracks were gradually removed. As soon as the 1941 Cadillac gets out of the way, No. 6 line car 152 will turn off Market Street onto Haight Street. The L car waits at the stop for the No. 6 to clear. A city emergency hospital ambulance is parked in front of a bait shop that would much later be transformed into the trendy Zuni Café. (Photograph by John Gerrard Graham; SFPL AAX0148.)

Basking in the autumn sun in 1948 at Potrero Yard, painter Heine Rist adds the finishing touches to coach 0383. (Courtesy of Charles Figone.)

Between 1944 and 1949, Muni took possession of over 369 new gas motor coaches from the White Motor Company. The 10 coaches, shown above on Harrison Street beside Garfield Square in August 1946, were painted in the gold and blue scheme that was introduced before the war. The coach being "pulled" out of its boxcar by Muni's general manager William Scott and other officials arrived in the latest "green and cream wings" scheme but without numbers. (Above, SFMR D5130; below, SFMR X1644_2.)

The many new buses needed new garages to augment the Market Street Railway facility at Twenty-fourth and Utah Streets. In 1948, Muni constructed a bus-servicing facility for the new Ocean Division on the site of the old Elkton yard, and in 1950, it opened Kirkland Division at North Point and Powell Streets. The arrival of White buses sounded the death knell for streetcar service on the Balboa, Fillmore, Haight, Hayes, McAllister, Mission, and Sutter Street lines. On the occasion of a parade of 55 new buses up Market Street on June 4, 1948, they took the "inside track," the former Market Street Railway domain. (SFMR X1684.)

It's all over! On July 3, 1948, ex-United Railroads and Market Street Railway car 439 (renumbered from 139 to avoid confusion with the Muni car of the same number) entered the Funston "bone yard" on Lincoln Way. Some of the former Haight cars, like this one, saw further duty on Mission Street. Note also that the last conductor on Haight Street was a woman. Shown at left on July 7, a No. 7 Haight bus passes car 439, parked where it pulled in four days before. (Above, BAERA 20299; below, SFMR X1750.)

Muni purchased more trolley coaches to use on its conversion of the Union Street line and replaced Market Street Railway trolley coaches on the pioneer No. 33 Eighteenth Street–Park line. In 1947, fifteen additional St. Louis Car Company buses entered service. They had been ordered but were not able to be delivered during the war. Here, coach 511 navigates the famous Clayton Street and Market Street U-turn on a test trip. Utilizing money left over from the reserve fund from Market Street Railway's 2¢ fare hike in 1938, Muni purchased two-dozen 40-passenger coaches from the Marmon-Herrington Company in Indiana. Below, 542 is posed on Union and Mason Streets with car 507. (Above, SFMR X1225B; below, SFMR X1698.)

Another part of the reserve fund was used for the purchase of 10 double-ended Presidents' Conference Cars (PCC), numbered 1006-1015, which arrived in late summer 1948. At left, newly arrived car 1010 is shown no later than September 6, 1948 (the last day the Portland Beavers played San Francisco that year). Used to the fresh air of open platforms, many conductors, like Sutro conductor L.R. Delaney (below left), may have found sedentary life on the new PCCs to be somewhat drafty. Below right, note the newspaper stuffed into the incompletely closed window behind Geary conductor Al Nielsen, who probably cannot believe that he is actually now permitted to sit on a leather cushioned seat to do his duties. (Left, photograph by John Gerrard Graham, SFPL AAX0004; below left, SFMR X1491; below right, SFMR X3476A.)

During the postwar period of consolidation, the *Trolley Topics* employee newsletter played a key role in building the identity of the "modern Muni." Besides introducing the employees to other operating divisions and marking the milestones of the modernization program under way, it announced important route changes, construction projects, and innovative employee recognition programs, like the "Courtesy Citation" and "Muni Man of the Month," which continues to this day. Adeline "Addy" Svendsen (above left) was its editor. She is seen demonstrating the controls of Muni's first foot-controlled Presidents' Conference Car. Photographer Marshall Moxom's and graphic artist Charles Reed's talents gave the magazine a professional look. One issue after her departure, publication of this rather advanced communication tool was suspended in September 1952. (Above left, SFMR Collection; above center and right, SFRA Grant Ute Collection.)

In 1949, the Potrero car house was converted to serve as garage and shop for trolley coaches. The yard area from York Street to Bryant Street, originally purchased for a general shops site but used as a track and pole storage yard, was paved, and wires were strung over it for outside storage of buses. The track areas inside were modernized and better lit to provide all manner of servicing from running maintenance to carpentry repairs. Below, Potrero Shop carpenter Henry Ute, an uncle of author Grant Ute, fabricates new doors for a "Baby Marmon," which were the only type of buses in the fleet with outward-opening doors. As such they were vulnerable to damage if opened into poles or fire hydrants near the curb. Both photographs were taken October 26, 1949. (Above, SFMR X2171; below, X2178.)

In the 1948 reconstruction of Muni, trolley buses became a major component of the fleet. Being a producer of cheap electric power, the San Francisco Public Utilities Commission (PUC) replaced streetcars on Muni's hilly Union Street line with trolley buses that could outperform motor coaches. With dynamic braking and light aluminum construction, one 140-horsepower electric motor could propel 100 passengers up the steepest hills, as a March 20, 1950, demonstration with coach 742 showed. (SFMR X2259B.)

Throughout the 1948 conversion of the Hayes, Haight, Fillmore, and McAllister Street lines and the 1949 conversion of the Balboa, Market, Mission, and Sutter Street lines, motor and trolley coaches introduced curbside loading all over San Francisco, as exemplified above by 0350 at California and Market Streets and below by 0196 at Mission and Eighteenth Streets. Convenient and safer for passengers, it did create traffic problems with coaches pulling into and out of traffic. (Above, BAERA 47222; below, BAERA 47221.)

Until trolley bus wires were strung on Market Street, just-out-of-the-boxcar motor coaches prowled this main thoroughfare. This September 30, 1948, scene also features a brand new Muni "torpedo" 1006 at center, advertising the release of the movie *Red River*. (SFMR X1828.)

In March 19, 1950, two stalwart remnants of the Panama-Pacific International Exposition service were discontinued—the D Van Ness-Geary and the H Potrero lines. Here, D car 14 crosses Ruger Street just inside Presidio Street, near Lyon and Greenwich Streets. Soon it will close out 35 years of service on a line built to celebrate San Francisco's rebirth. (Photograph by John Gerrard Graham; SFPL AAX0148.)

After the war, the Muni finally accomplished its 1914 goal of extending the F Stockton to the Southern Pacific Railroad Depot. Later, it extended it further by looping back to Second and Market Streets to eliminate the Market Street Railway No. 41 line service. In the sunlight of a late autumn afternoon, car 28 travels across Market Street from Fourth Street to Stockton Street. By October 1951, the F was discontinued. (Photograph by John Gerrard Graham; SFPL AAX0179.)

During the spring and summer of 1949, a second trolley coach yard was constructed behind the Geary car house at Presidio and Post Streets. It would serve the No. 1 California; the No. 3 Jackson; the No. 5 Fulton; No. 21 Hayes; the newly numbered 30 Stockton, formerly the F car line; and part of the No. 41 Union, formerly the E car line. These pictures show the results of 167 days of construction between March 26 and September 8. (Above, SFMR D5548; below, SFMR D5602.)

There is a certain casualness to San Francisco by the middle of the 20th century—note the Buick fearlessly making a left turn from the curb lane at Post and Market Streets on October 26, 1951. The Crocker Building in the center has since been razed; the bank building across the street from it, on the corner of Post and Montgomery Streets, had all but the bottom stories removed and is now a Wells Fargo Bank branch. (BAERA 7057.)

While the trolley and motor coach fleet was essentially brand new, this early-September 1949 view shows the contrast between the bus and streetcar fleets. With the exception of 15 modern cars, Muni streetcars date from 1912 to 1927. A remnant two-man crew law, which hampered Market Street Railway 10 years before, now makes streetcars cost ineffective. As a result, motor coach service was substituted on nights and weekends wherever feasible. (SFMR Collection.)

By the date of this July 7, 1949, photograph, Market Street has been converted to a three-lane thoroughfare where streetcars rule the center lane and electric trolley and motor coaches (not seen here) ply the curb lane, leaving the middle one for other traffic. Cheap reliable service via Muni keeps theaters and the retail stores, such as Kress, Penney's, Hales, Emporium, and Woolworth's, between Mason and Stockton Streets vibrant. (SFMR X2101.)

The two scenes on this page and the previous one were taken seconds apart. Compare this image to the 1917 view located on the top of page 50, before the installation of the outer tracks. (SFMR X2099.)

Just a few months into the program, in May 1951, however, the Muni Man of the Month was indeed a woman—Ethyl Rutland. She was a conductor and 10-year veteran of the L Taraval. (SFMR X2733.)

While competition in the form of the Market Street Railway was gone, Muni found itself competing against the private automobile after the war. As wartime industry waned, revenues fell and there were immediate pressures to increase fare-box revenues. Muni raised its base fare in 1946 to 10¢. To retain riders, management stressed the courtesy of platform crews who, as today, were the public face of Muni. Management also emphasized appearance, and an innovative employee recognition program allowed the public to recommend outstanding employees for Courtesy Citations. This soon evolved into the Muni Man of the Month award program, with the transit advertising company awarding a $50-a-month cash award to the chosen employee. (SFMR X1425.)

In 1951, the Muni's last independent competitor, the California Street Cable Railroad Company, went out of business after it was unable to pay its liability insurance. On the last day of operation, July 31, 1951, Cal Cable car 1 (chalk marked "Hyde Street Only") climbs California Street on one of its last trips. That very day, Muni management changed as general manager William Scott retired and turned over the leadership to Charles Miller, a Market Street Railway career employee. (SFMR X2815A.)

As 1951 ended, San Francisco received the very last order of PCC cars produced for an American street railway when cars 1016–1040 arrived. While built for two-man crews, these cars would usher in the retirement of the 1912 Arnold cars and several of the most deteriorated 1914 Battleships. It would also mark the end of the period of reconstruction. Both 1016 and 1040 survive to this day, having been restored in 2010 and 2011. Car 1016 was restored to its original two-man configuration by the Bay Area Electric Railroad Association's Western Railway Museum, and 1040 was restored for F line service by the Muni. (BAERA 45657.)

OPPOSITE: San Francisco's topography had always worked in the favor of its public transit carriers. But with more powerful automobiles, people had to be coaxed to use the municipal railway. This was the era of the family automobile, emerging traffic congestion, and a phenomenon called "gridlock." To combat this, Muni began a public information campaign to encourage use of public transit. On January 26, 1955, motor coach 0379 displays an advertising placard touting it as a solution to traffic jams. (BAERA 47223.)

RATIONALIZATION
1952–1963

After the war, Mayor Roger Lapham had proposed replacing the cable cars by introducing twin-engine "hill climbing" motor buses. In 1947, this provoked a firestorm of protest and galvanized public sentiment on behalf of the cable system, taking politicians by surprise and resulting in the protection of the Powell Street lines. By 1952, though, Muni's last competitor, the California Street Cable Railroad Company, was incorporated into the system. With that step, all transit services in San Francisco were under the aegis of the municipal railway—including the Cal Cable's O'Farrell, Jones & Hyde Street and California Street lines. Meanwhile, Muni's plant and vehicles had been modernized with the addition of 40 modern streetcars, 365 trolley coaches, and 379 motor buses.

Elmer Robinson was inaugurated as mayor, and San Francisco's business interests were anticipating a period of economic growth led by consumer spending. This was a time of freeway building, redevelopment, and working condition changes. Having just converted many old Market Street Railway and original Muni lines to trolley or motor coach service, two-man streetcar service was limited and eventually phased out during this period. A second "Cable Car War" broke out over the fate of the California Street Cable Railroad Company properties, which resulted in the demise of the O'Farrell-Jones Streets line and the sudden abandonment of the Washington-Jackson Streets line. At the end of a decade of rationalization of its services, Muni celebrated its golden anniversary in a big way.

TRAFFIC JAMS CAN BE REDUCED
1 BUS = 35 PRIVATE AUTOMOBILES
IF PASSENGERS CARRIED

Led by society matron Friedel Klussman, shown above left in 1948 inspecting the workings of the cable car turntable at Powell and Market Streets, a coalition emerged and successfully defeated the plan to eliminate the cable cars. By 1954, though, retail merchants demanded parking and lobbied to eliminate the cable car on O'Farrell Street to allow various streets to become one-way to access new garages. In a June 1954 election, two ballot measures competed to "save the cable cars." Klussman's proposition J was defeated through what some supporters described as a disinformation campaign. This resulted in the elimination not only of the O'Farrell, Jones & Hyde Streets lines but also, as retaliation, the Washington & Jackson Streets line that was never considered for abandonment. Leading the protest on May 15, 1954, author Philip Hoffman was front and center on the roof of the last Hyde Street car 51. Author Robert Townley can also be seen in the Air Force uniform on the steps. (Above left, SFMR X2066; below left, SFPL AAC8063; above, courtesy of Philip Hoffman.)

VOTE "YES" ON "N"

Free Muni Carmen From 6 Day Week

Muni Carmen, chained together like convicts, create a sensation on Market Street. Carmen spent their one day off reminding voters they are still chained to a six day week, while all other civil service employees work five!

THE FIVE DAY WEEK WILL MEAN BETTER AND SAFER SERVICE

The 5 Day Week is the American Way

VOTE "YES" ON "N"

San Francisco 5 day week committee

With surplus midday crews and equipment, one Muni innovation was operating reduced fare "Shopper's Shuttles" through the downtown and Mission shopping districts. A 5¢ fare was adopted to encourage ridership, one-third of the standard 15¢ fare adopted in 1951. On November 12, 1954, at Ocean Yard, prewar coach 060 and postwar coach 0213 show the route's distinctive yellow route signs and flags. (SFMR X3505.)

In 1955, Muni carmen were still working six days a week but campaigning for a five-day workweek. Following the passage of the one-man car ordinance in 1954, allowing streetcars to operate without a conductor, the citizens voted in November 1955 to allow a five-day workweek. (Courtesy of Art Curtis.)

In the initial days of its one-man service on March 14, 1955, PCC 1028 meets two-man car 178 at Forest Hill Station in the Twin Peaks Tunnel. With the elimination of the two-man car requirement the prior year, the PCCs could be easily converted to more economical one-man service. The 1938 one-man prohibition, which crippled the Market Street Railway's profitability, came back to haunt the Muni and probably contributed to the discontinuance of streetcar service on Stockton and Mission Streets. The latter Mission rail corridor had relatively new track. Currently, 1028 is being stored for potential rehabilitation. Car 178 was preserved by the Bay Area Electric Railroad Association and still runs, looking as it does in this picture. (SFMR X3553.)

Running as a training car in 1956, car 1018 pauses outbound on Market Street at Octavia Street under the Central Skyway construction site. Nature retired this visual eyesore 33 years later with the Loma Prieta earthquake, which also wiped out the sister Embarcadero Freeway (see page 129). (Photograph by John Gerrard Graham; SFPL AAX0191.)

In the mid-1950s, city planners drew a bead on the Western Addition and, in the context of the freeway mania sweeping the state, sketched up plans for a Geary Expressway linking downtown to the Golden Gate Bridge. The B Geary Street and California Street car lines were the only things in their way. In 1956, the heavily traveled B was slated for conversion to bus service. With this, the Muni could retire the two-man cars and replace many of the early White motor coaches. Unable to pass bond measures to buy equipment, the city leased new buses from the Mack Truck Company. The first coaches arrived in November 1955 and, shortly thereafter, were displayed at the Civic Center. (SFMR X3662.)

On Christmas Eve 1956, the B line has just five more days to run. Along with the Geary Street cars, the birdcage signal and Gene Compton's cafeteria are gone. The Handlery Motor Inn replaced the Stewart Hotel in 1964, and the Milton Kreis Restaurant is now an art gallery. Only the Powell cable and the St. Francis Hotel endure. (BAERA 45102.)

Few city blocks have changed more than this one at Geary Street and Van Ness Avenue. After the Geary Street cars were discontinued on December 29, 1956, the two top floors of Tommy's Joynt were removed—literally "sliced before your eyes." The used car lot is now an office building, and the site of St. Mary's Cathedral, which was destroyed by fire in 1962, is now a television station. (Courtesy of Clark Frazier.)

The shop crew celebrated the end of the Geary Street lines and the closing of Geary Street barn on the evening of December 29, 1956, with "Muni Malts" on board Muni car 1 and ex–Market Street Railway 578. The latter car had been restored earlier that year for the 50th anniversary of the 1906 earthquake and fire and is part of Muni's historic fleet today. These would be the last cars to vacate the barn in 1959. (SFMR X3829A.)

On October 4, 1957, Marmon-Herrington trolley coach 837 climbs Union Street between Taylor and Jones Streets with Coit Tower and the Bay Bridge on the skyline. One has to wonder if Muni's sign campaign on the bus dash, which was meant to encourage ridership, actually had a paradoxical effect on recruitment. (SFMR M151.)

Shown at right, the 1939 White 061 provided No. 39 line service to Coit Tower from 1939 into the early 1970s. (SFMR X4005.)

After the elimination of streetcar service on Geary Street, Muni's next order of business was to retire all of the remaining original two-man "Iron Monster" cars on May 9, 1958. Committed to routing through O'Shaughnessy's tunnels and private right-of-ways, the five surviving lines (J, K, L, M, and N) would require more PCCs. No longer in production but with many surplus cars around the country, San Francisco turned to the St. Louis Public Service Company (SLPS) and lease-purchased 66 (later 70) used cars (remodeled and painted to Muni specifications) for $9,000 each, payable at $1,000 per year for nine years. Five years into the deal, a public entity took over the private SLPS and offered Muni the cars for $100 each to get out of the lease. As a result, San Francisco paid $6,100 each for the cars that were the backbone of its fleet over the next quarter century. This compared to the $42,000 each that it paid for the 25 new PCCs ordered in 1951. Pictured above on August 12, 1957, the first cars were delivered by rail via the Southern Pacific's old main line, the route of Interstate 280 today. Conductor Albert Fleiger (right) checks his time with motorman Tony Marelich. It will be their and car 181's last trip. (Above, BAERA 49870; left, courtesy of Art Curtis.)

Mayor George Christopher took credit for bringing the New York Giants to town in 1958. They played the first two seasons at Seals Stadium along the No. 22 Fillmore Street line. Shown above, note the second set of wires that allowed baseball "trippers" to be parked and not block the line. Christopher also took time out to support "Ride the Muni Week" on October 30, 1958, by actually riding to city hall from his home near St. Francis Circle on PCC 1107. "Mr. Muni" himself, bus driver Edward Mullane, accompanies him. (Above, SFMR X4377; below, SFMR X4135_2.)

As soon as Candlestick Park opened in April 1960, the 25 forty-passenger Baby Marmon trolley coaches, bought right after the war, were surplus. They were stored in, of all places, the Palace of Fine Arts—itself waiting its first restoration in 1961. Despite their short life and limited usefulness, three of these buses have been preserved in museums. (BAERA 51664.)

Day games in the new Candlestick Park drew transit resources to the isolated southeastern corner of the city and away from the downtown service need. These pictures were taken on opening day at Candlestick, April 12, 1960. With narrow streets and limited access to Third Street, it was apparent from the beginning that Candlestick service was going to be a major league headache for Muni. (Above, SFMR X5578; below, SFMR X5579.)

In 1962, Muni celebrated its 50th anniversary in style. Even Muni's old nemesis, the Park Department, did a planting to commemorate the event at the Conservatory of Flowers. (SFMR X7529A.)

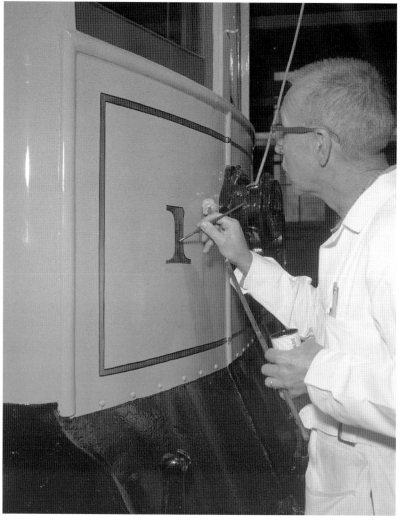

Led by a civic group, including cable car advocate Friedel Klussman, the celebration's highlight was the restoration of car 1 to its original 1912 appearance. Elkton Paint Shop foreman Walter Blake applies the paint, gold leaf, and varnish to the car's number. For a week in October, Muni operated it along Market Street with 5¢ fares—justified as part of the Shopper's Shuttle route. (SFMR X7490.)

The event also included corporate-decorated cable cars, an expanded bell ringing contest, and painting the only Mack without dents into a "Golden Coach," complete with a red carpet and bar. (SFMR X7527.)

Veteran Muni motorman Al Millar (right), wearing his original badge and customary silk scarf, and conductor Tony Campagna, wearing his California Street Cable Railroad badges, ran car 1 on its daily route from East Bay Terminal to Eleventh and Market Streets. Each star on Campagna's sleeve represents five years of service. (SFMR X7511_5.)

Here is Market Street looking east from Fourth Street as it appeared during Muni's Golden Week on October 15, 1962. At this time, the J Church Street line was served exclusively by "Baby 10s," like 1033 pictured here, while the 1100s were used on the tunnel lines K, L, M, and N. The Roos-Atkins men's store would move across the street before going out of business many years later. (SFMR X7513_4.)

On November 18, 1963, Muni staged this "roar of the four" shot at the foot of Taraval Street. In this setting, the year's "Muni Men" winners could hear the roar of the surf behind St. Louis Car Company–built trolley coach 884, PCC 1016, motorized cable car 62, and Mack coach 2518. The nearest trolley bus wires were 2.5 miles away at the end of Fulton Street. (SFMR X8275.)

Fageol Twin Coach 639 turns off Market Street onto McAllister Street, while an ex–St. Louis Public Service Company 1143 stops at the safety island on March 7, 1962. This image also shows the mid-Market area when the Paramount Theater was still open. Between 1967 and 1973, Market Street was in a continuous state of disruption. (SFMR X7045.)

OPPOSITE: Car 1148 negotiates its way across the temporary elevated trackage at Collingwood Street on September 11, 1973, before dropping down into the Twin Peaks Tunnel at Eureka Valley Station. All of the buildings at this site still stand. (BAERA 50789.)

PART OF A LARGER WHOLE
1964–1977

At the time of Muni's Golden Week in October 1962, it was clear that San Francisco was part of a larger metropolitan area, including Contra Costa, Alameda, Marin, and San Mateo Counties. No longer linked by ferryboats or even the San Francisco-Oakland Bay Bridge Railway, it was time to address regional mass transportation needs. Preliminary studies recommended the creation of a Bay Area Rapid Transit (BART) District, which was funded in 1962 by a $792 million bond issue approved by voters of Alameda, Contra Costa, and San Francisco Counties (with Marin and San Mateo Counties choosing not to participate). The plan included a multilevel subway on Market Street and for a Muni line from the Ferry Building to St. Francis Circle, connecting via the Twin Peaks Tunnel. BART would significantly influence Muni's service over the succeeding years. Despite some of its equipment reaching midlife around this time, Muni functioned with remarkable reliability. However, equipment, personnel, and passenger loyalty would be severely tested by a number of construction projects, such as the BART subway, built on Market and Mission Streets, and the reconstruction of the decrepit cable car system.

Bion Arnold had envisioned an eventual subway on Market Street in his original Muni plan. The city engineer's design of the Twin Peaks Tunnel also included a station at Eureka Valley (just west of Castro Street) that would serve as a stop in a future Market Street subway. Connecting the metro subway to the Twin Peaks Tunnel while still operating was a tremendous challenge, as seen in this October 17, 1973, photograph of the "Collingwood Street El." Cars had to be temporarily routed over the Castro Street station, which was being constructed underneath. (SFMR M1637_2.)

During BART construction, sections of Market Street were planked over with wood and steel plates. In this picture, taken on March 21, 1968, members of the Muni "freshman classes" of 1948 (1006) and 1949 (712) are seen rumbling over the Montgomery Street Station, which was then under construction. The rough changing roadways on Market Street destroyed the suspension systems of much of the Twin Coach trolley coach fleet, requiring redeployment of some Marmon-Herringtons, like 712 from Potrero to the Presidio Division. The 712 would remain in service for another nine years, and a rebuilt 1006 still crosses this intersection on the historic F line today. (Photograph by Norman Rolfe; BAERA 49676.)

There is something both old and new in this December 23, 1967, view, looking east on Market Street at Geary Street. Rails from Geary Street seem to allow "ghost cars" to enter Market Street, while PCCs operate on temporary "outer tracks" that moved into the curb lanes to avoid BART construction. Here, an inbound 1100 appears to be running on the wrong side of the street at New Montgomery Street. (Photograph by Norman Rolfe, BAERA 49756.)

In the 1950s, the Ferry Building became a hidden part of the city's transit past after the two-level Embarcadero Freeway blocked it from view. In the 1950s, Muni's ferry terminal was relocated to a paved lot on the Embarcadero, north of Mission Street. Today, the nonprofit Market Street Railway's San Francisco Railway Museum is housed in a boutique hotel, located just south of this site. (Loring Jensen Collection, BAERA 51666.)

Meanwhile, on the other end of the tunnel, the classic West Portal facade was sacrificed in order to accommodate a multiple-car train platform. On December 26, 1976, workers are demolishing the tunnel to allow for the new station. The West Portal School appears intact in the photograph, taken before its eastern wing was razed. A year later, workers were busy constructing the new canopy for the West Portal Station, while PCC cars, like 1109, ran underneath. (Above, photograph by Norman Rolfe, BAERA 51284; below, SFMR M2462_8.)

BART construction under Market Street resulted in frequent delays, affecting schedules and service reliability. Streetcars were detoured off upper Market Street, west of Dolores, via Duboce, Church, and Seventeenth Streets to extend the Muni Metro Subway to Castro. In order to accommodate the resulting increase in running times, Muni purchased 11 worn out Toronto Transit Commission PCCs. Shown above left on December 24, 1973, several of them were in the old Elkton Shops having their trucks re-gauged. Encroached upon by the Balboa Park BART Station and literally falling down, the United Railroads' "temporary" 1907 shops were finally razed in May 1977 to make way for a modern maintenance facility for the rail fleet. (Above left, BAERA 51483; above right, SFMR M2370_2.)

Muni's inspector corps is essential to keeping service on schedule. Art Curtis (fourth row, fifth from right) was the afternoon inspector at Van Ness Avenue and Market Street during BART construction and would arrange up to 75 switches of cars and 25 car trades a shift to get the evening runs back on time. This required cooperation from crews who would be told to "keep your eye out for a car leaving the beach on your time." On page 106, Curtis, who retired as chief inspector after a career spanning 37 years, can be seen as a teenager standing behind the motorman of the last two-man car in May 1958. (Courtesy of Art Curtis.)

Having established an "exact fare" policy after the murder of an operator during a robbery attempt in 1968, another fare innovation was the introduction of the Fast Pass in May 1974. Only cable car conductors continued to collect cash fares directly—a tradition that continues today. Here, Muni general manager Curtis Green accepts $11 from supervisor Harvey Milk, a champion of the Fast Pass, in front of a newly arrived Boeing Articulated Light Rail Vehicle, designed for metro operation. (SFMR Y870820_B7.)

Bus driver turned inspector in the mid-1960s, Curtis Green was an example of the talented postwar employees who rose to later manage the railway. He became the Muni's first African American inspector just weeks after being recognized as "Muni Man of the Month" in June 1963. Advancing rapidly through the ranks, he became general manager in July 1974 and directed the system during eight tumultuous years of planning, construction, and change through the opening of the Muni Metro system. His poster mate, George Martensen, retired after 36 years of safe driving with no avoidable accident on his record. He gained some notoriety a few years earlier as the operator of a bus chartered to the Mitchell brothers who filmed an X-rated scene aboard. When queried by management why he did not realize what was going on in the rear of coach 2352, Martensen simply replied that he was keeping his eyes on the road. (Courtesy of Art Curtis.)

32 YEARS OF SERVICE AND COURTESY
Curtis E. Green, 39 (left) and George J. Martensen, 36 (right) have, between them, given over 32 years of service to their friends and passengers on at least a half-dozen lines of the Municipal Railway. Green, 144th "Muni Man of the Month", with the Muni since 1945, is an operator on the No. 19-Polk line. He has added 11 Safe Driving Awards and 10 consecutive years of accident free bus operation to his personnel record.
George Martensen, 145th "Muni Man" has been with the Railway for 14 years, an operator on the No. 38-Geary line for the past four and has also compiled a record of 10 consecutive years of accident free operation. He is a five-time runner up in the "Muni Man" contest.

Reflecting wider social trends of the era, there were major changes in Muni's workforce. By 1974, the "men only" requirement for operator positions was eliminated and tradeswomen joined shop crews, as the May 1, 1975, photograph of mechanics Beverly Martin, left, and Helen Carson, right, documents. Evelyn Wells is pictured below on May 23, 1979, shortly after she became the first female inspector. (Above, SFMR T0087_A; below, SFMR T0095_4.)

San Francisco's transit workers have been unionized since 1901. A group of union officials meet with soon-to-be general manager Curtis Green (second row, second from right) in 1973 at Washington-Mason Division. Union president John T. Squire is in the center of the first row. In addition to the 1934 General Strike, Muni has had only three work stoppages since 1912, which include the following: 1946, 1952, and a sympathy strike, when all city crafts workers walked out in 1974. The Golden Gate Bridge, Mount Tamalpais, Pier 43, and the *Balclutha* are visible below behind the strike-bound Kirkland Yard on the afternoon of April 30, 1974. (Above, SFMR Collection; below, SFMR M2197_3.)

Postwar trolley coaches had exceeded their useful lives by the late 1960s. Still running in February 1975, twenty-six-year-old Marmon-Herrington 679 (above) glides down Castro Street nearing the end not only of the No. 8 Market Street line but also of its own service life. Following the successful testing of two prototypes from Canada, an order was placed in 1974 for 343 trolley coaches from Flyer Industries. Former demonstrator 5002 (right) is turning from Union Street onto Van Ness Avenue on the electrified No. 45 Greenwich, which had replaced the old D line. (Above, courtesy of John Bromley; right, courtesy of Cameron Beach.)

By 1969, Muni was suffering from several years of under-funding and aging infrastructure. No manufacturer of any of its nearly 1,000 vehicles was still in business. There was no local source of funding available to replace old buses, some of which dated back to the years before World War II. Under Public Utilities Commission direction, Muni formed the San Francisco Municipal Railway Improvement Corporation (SFMRIC) and received funding for 400 replacement motor coaches, including V-8 engines, three-speed transmissions, and engine brakes. On June 24, 1969, brand new GMC 3012 enters San Francisco for the first time via the Bay Bridge. (SFMR M639_10.)

In 1975, Muni also secured 100 thirty-five-foot coaches from the AM General Corporation of Indiana. They were purchased to be used on short "community service" lines that had narrower streets. Here, 4172 rumbles along the Embarcadero in front of the old facade of Pier 39, later to be transformed into a major San Francisco tourist destination. (SFMR M2340_5.)

In the early 1970s, anticipating the completion of the metro, Muni joined with Boston's Massachusetts Bay Transportation Authority in replacing aging PCCs. With the demise of the streetcar industry, there were very few American builders of rail transit vehicles at the time. With federal monies flowing, a "United States Standard Light Rail Vehicle" (LRV) was designed for both fleets to be capable of operating in a subway and on streets. Muni officials gather on October 26, 1977, in the Muni Metro yard to inspect two new cars that had just arrived from the Boeing-Vertol Corporation. (SFMR M2434_1.)

Shown above on January 31, 1978, Mayor George Moscone is seen sitting in the cab of one of the new cars. It was not until almost four years later, on September 19, 1982, that the PCCs would be retired . . . for a time. (M2477_9.)

In 1978, with new leadership and a revitalized planning department, Muni began a planning process as bold and far-reaching as that of Bion Arnold. Recognizing that Muni was dedicating almost 75 percent of its service to downtown, which constituted only 33 percent of its passenger trips, its planners soon designed a system responsive to the city's changing travel patterns. This brought about the first effort to move San Francisco from a radial to a modified grid route structure—a step that had eluded the railway since O'Shaughnessy's failed attempt to extend the A line across Golden Gate Park to serve the isolated Inner Sunset. One of the first changes was to extend the No. 28 Nineteenth Avenue line through the Presidio to directly link the Marina to the Richmond and Sunset Districts for the first time. In February 1974, No. 28 line coach 3166 passes the Golden Gate Bridge on the Presidio's Lincoln Boulevard, shown above. Planners also attempted to speed up running times by designing "streetcar only" lanes on Judah Street and "bulb" loading zones. Flxible coach 4008, one of the 10 ordered in 1969, boards passengers at a zone at Polk and California Streets on June 6, 1974. (Above, photograph by Frank Lichtanski, courtesy of Jim Husing; below, SFMR M1853_2.)

In 1982, the entire cable car system was shut down for a complete rebuilding, including a rehabilitation of the historic Ferries and Cliff House Railroad car and powerhouse at Washington and Mason Streets. The 1972 Transamerica Pyramid stands sentinel over the 1887 cable carbarn. Compare this view of the building to that of the morning of the 1906 earthquake on page 11. (Courtesy of Walter Vielbaum.)

Another major service innovation was the electrification of several more lines, including the No. 24 Divisadero and the No. 55 Sacramento Street lines. A portion of the latter traversed Andrew Hallidie's original cable car route. Motor coaches had struggled on these hilly routes since cable abandonment in the early 1940s. Shop crews had to be regularly stationed at the end of the No. 55 line to refill transmission fluid that had foamed out on the Sacramento Street trips. In December 1981, trolley coaches overcame the Nob Hill grades, as seen here. Within six weeks, the No. 55 was combined with the No. 1 California, providing through service from the Golden Gateway to outer Richmond. In 1983, the No. 24 Divisadero was electrified after being extended south to Third Street to become a major crosstown line. (SFMR Collection.)

In 1985, Muni acquired its first articulated motor coaches, whose addition had been envisioned in the 1979 five-year plan. These German MAN Corporation buses were used on heavily traveled routes on Geary Street, Mission Street, Third Street, and the Downtown Loop. In September 1985, coach 6000 leaves Fremont and Mission Streets on the No. 42 Downtown Loop line, which connected the Caltrain depot to the Central Business District, North Beach, Fisherman's Wharf, and Van Ness Avenue. Today, everything in this picture is gone—the Bridge Terminal approach, the office building, and the buses. (Photograph by Will Whittaker; courtesy of Walter Vielbaum.)

In 1991, Muni received its first articulated trolley coaches from Flyer Industries. They were immediately assigned to the No. 31 Balboa Street line that had recently been electrified and extended to the beach—fulfilling one of O'Shaughnessy's route proposals from 50 years before. Even though the No. 31 line did not warrant articulated coaches, its previous diesel bus service had been handicapped accessible. Since the new trolley coaches were the only ones with wheelchair lifts, they had to be used on the route. In May 1994, Flyer articulated coach 7010 passed the entrance to the University of San Francisco's Lone Mountain campus on Turk Street at Chabot Terrace. (SFMR Y940504_20.)

On November 16, 1989, forty Muni buses were also put into service from the East Bay Terminal to Yerba Buena Island so people could walk to inspect the repairs to the Bay Bridge, which had a section of its upper deck collapse. (SFMR Y891129_36A.)

On October 19, 1989, the Loma Prieta earthquake struck the Bay Area during a World Series game between both Bay Area teams. The Embarcadero Freeway was severely damaged, and a similar structure in Oakland collapsed with loss of life. As a result, the freeway had to be razed, opening up the waterfront. Flyer coach 4566 provides Embarcadero line service just a couple of days after the disaster. (SFMR Collection.)

After the "wars" of 1947 and 1954 galvanized local and national attention on the cable cars, they had become iconic symbols of San Francisco in the hearts of its citizens and increasing tourist trade. Television personalities, performers, international leaders, and celebrities, including astronauts, were to be photographed on San Francisco's most unique form of transit. Singer Tony "I Left My Heart in San Francisco" Bennett seemed to be enjoying Mayor Diane Feinstein's company aboard California Street car 58 in 1984. When the Giants moved to their new ballpark at Mission Bay in 2000, a retired cable car was renumbered "24" and "44" on alternate sides to honor Giants' greats Willie Mays and Willie McCovey. Shown being hoisted above McCovey Cove to its current center field installation, the iconic cable car was an immediate "splash hit" with fans. (Above, SFMR Y840501; below, SFMR Collection.)

On September 19, 1982, the day LRVs replaced the last PCCs, buses replaced cable cars for a complete two-year system rebuilding. While San Franciscans might have to tolerate life without streetcars on the surface of Market Street, the hospitality industry would not tolerate the city's diminished marketability without cable cars. Muni's 1979 five-year plan had proposed a historic streetcar fleet running to Fisherman's Wharf and Fort Mason. Leveraging this existing plan, the not-for-profit Market Street Railway emerged to champion an experimental historic car operation to run on the surface tracks on Market Street during the summer tourist season of 1983. The San Francisco Chamber of Commerce provided support, and the San Francisco Historic Trolley Festival was born—and with it an American streetcar renaissance. From left to right, Mayor Diane Feinstein, chamber of commerce president Gordon Swanson, volunteer San Francisco Historic Trolley Festival manager Rick Laubscher, and Muni instructor Reno Bini share the inauguration of the trolley festival at the Bridge Terminal on May 27, 1983. (Courtesy of Rick Laubscher.)

Running San Francisco is a "hands-on" job. Mayor Feinstein has car 1 "on the brass"—the controller's fastest point. (SFMR Y850518B_19.)

A variety of cars—Muni's car 1, PCCs, an LRV, as well as foreign imports— are on display at Fifth Avenue and Market Street. (SFMR Y920412.)

Bay Area Electric Railroad Association's restored 1923 Muni "Iron Monster" car 178 and Muni's 1914 Battleship car 130, which had been restored prior to the festival, are bookends for venerable car 1. These cars formed the backbone of the festival fleet augmented by a number of vintage cars from around the world. Blackpool England "boat car" 228 turns at the Seventeenth Street and Noe Street terminus; it was an immediate hit with riders. Bechtel Engineering, one of the original Bay Bridge construction contractors, had donated the funds to pay for the shipping of the boat car in 1984. (Right, courtesy of Rick Laubscher; below, SFMR Y860902_11a.)

Ex-Philadelphia PCC 1050 waits for Muni 162 to make a test run after the latter was purchased back from a Southern California railway museum by the Market Street Railway, Muni's not-for-profit partner for historic fleet operation. PCC 1052 is one of 14 ex-Philadelphia PCCs painted in different schemes reminiscent of PCC operations in other American cities. After being preliminarily restored by MSR volunteers, car 162 was finished in Muni's shops. (Courtesy of Kevin Sheridan.)

OPPOSITE: Muni required space behind its Embarcadero Station to properly store and turn cars. But the interests backing the Embarcadero Center prevailed in having the station as close to the Embarcadero as possible, resulting in the crossover being placed before the station. The arrangement made passengers wait, while the operator changed ends and slowed turning at one of the system's most critical loading points. This essentially re-created the pre-earthquake cable car turntable problem (see page 8) that the 1906 Ferry Loop addressed. The Muni Metro Turnback (MMT), built in the mid-1990s, finally solved the Embarcadero Terminal bottleneck. This view looks west toward the Embarcadero Muni Metro Station and shows the newly constructed tail tracks and crossover switches. (Courtesy of Walter Vielbaum.)

LEADING THE AMERICAN STREETCAR RENAISSANCE
1994–2012

The Bay Area Rapid Transit District's "gift" to the city had been the Market Street Subway and a BART line under Mission Street that would relieve Muni from providing express and limited stop service on Mission Street. But there were costs—including having to reimburse BART for each Muni Fast Pass used on BART trains within San Francisco. More significantly, the city had to accept a decision about the location of the Embarcadero Station that resulted in reestablishing a critical stub-end choke point at the foot of Market Street. After the demolition of the Embarcadero Freeway, the F Market and Wharves line was extended to Fisherman's Wharf by way of a roadway through a bold public place that became Ferry Plaza. Later, in the 1990s, Muni constructed an extension to the metro system with a route (called the MMX) to Caltrain Station, via the Embarcadero line, serving the Giants' new baseball stadium. Initially used by the N Judah Street line as far as the Caltrain terminal at Fourth and King Streets, it became the first leg of the T Third Street light rail line. The T line opened to the public in April 2007, returning streetcar service to Mission Bay, Dogpatch, the Bayview, and Visitacion Valley for the first time in 66 years. Using Muni in new ways, San Francisco has again shown America how streetcars can revitalize neighborhoods and enhance great public spaces.

Originally proposed in Muni's 1979 five-year plan and piloted in the San Francisco Historic Trolley Festival in 1983, the F Market line opened in 1995 as a permanent surface line on Market Street from Castro to the East Bay Terminal. After the demolition of the damaged Embarcadero Freeway, the route was extended to Fisherman's Wharf via the Ferry Building and a special Embarcadero right-of-way in 2000 and renamed F Market and Wharves. In addition to providing an inexpensive and fun tourist return trip from cable car rides, the F soon became a mainstay reliable surface back-up whenever metro operational and maintenance issues created delays in the subway. Car 1056, painted in Kansas City livery, is on break on the Embarcadero Station, south of Mission Street. The Muni's own 1010, painted in a blue and yellow scheme that pre-dated its 1948 arrival, makes a big splash on the Embarcadero's dedicated right-of-way. With large capacity, all but three of the original 10 cars have been restored for service. (Both, courtesy of Kevin Sheridan.)

Above, the popular Blackpool boat car passes the ferries and tour boats seen at Pier 43 with Alcatraz in the background. (Courtesy of Kevin Sheridan.)

Women had served as cable car conductors during the Korean War and World War II. Mary Alice Ball (above left) is congratulated by her gripman on being honored as "Muni Man of the Month" in February 1953. Women, however, were not permitted to ride on the outside steps of cable cars. In 1965, Mona Hutchins (below left) was arrested after refusing to move off cable car steps in act of civil disobedience. Photographed as "first girl to ride cable car steps," Hutchins was a conservative libertarian and an unlikely associate of Mario Savio and the "left-leaning" Berkeley Free Speech Movement. Her button reads, "I am a right-wing extremist." It was 33 more years before a woman, Fannie Mae Barnes (above right), qualified to grip a cable car in 1998. In January 2011, Willa Johnson and Cassandra Griffin (below right) formed an all-woman crew on the Hyde Street grip. (Above left, photograph by Robert Rockwell, SFMR Collection; above right, SFMR Y98601C_28; below left, SFMR M1867; below right, courtesy of Cameron Beach.)

Plagued with troubles from the start, the Boeing LRVs were retired before their planned life expectancy had run out. Their replacements were manufactured by Ansaldo Breda, an Italian firm that assembled them in San Francisco as a condition of the contract. The Breda cars were phased in over seven years from 1995 to 2002. These new LRVs could not be coupled to the Boeing cars and had different train control systems. During this period, there were many operational challenges running two fleets of incompatible cars—especially in the metro subway. Boeing LRVs are lined up at the metro yard named for former general manager Curtis Green. The Breda cars are shown during assembly. (Both, courtesy of Walter Vielbaum.)

With the Giants' move to Mission Bay, the team located along the extension of the metro line being prepared for Third Street rail service. On March 31, 2000, the stadium opened with a preseason night game, and for the first time since the H-line shut down 50 years before, Muni streetcars served a San Francisco ballpark. (SFMR Y2000412A_28.)

The T Third Street line opened up service to the new Mission Bay development, just south of the channel, and the formerly industrial—but now trendy—"Dog Patch" neighborhood. Off Third Street, Muni built an extensive metro east shop and yard facility. A group of Breda cars sit under sparkling yard lights. (Courtesy Kevin Sheridan.)

The T Third Street line extends all the way out Third Street to Visitacion Valley to the end of the old Market Street Railway No. 16 route. Upon the line opening in 2007, Muni finally had built a line to the Bayview and Hunter Point Districts—fulfilling community requests dating back to 1916. As in the Sunset District, a Muni line was once again a vehicle of development—this time providing neighborhood revitalization. The second phase of this project will be the Central Subway from Fourth and King Streets through the South of Market (SOMA) under Fourth and Stockton Streets by Union Square to Chinatown. It is expected to open in 2018. (Courtesy Kevin Sheridan.)

In an attempt to better coordinate policy and financial planning and ensure political independence and stability of governance for all transportation matters, in November 1999, the voters of San Francisco passed a charter amendment to establish a Municipal Transportation Agency to oversee the department of parking and traffic, city parking garages, and operation of taxis in addition to the operation of the San Francisco Municipal Railway. It instituted a proof-of-payment (POP) policy on rail lines and initiated a Transit Effectiveness Program to review, rationalize, and restructure routes for the first time in 30 years. It also approved the complete rehabilitation of Muni's car 1. During an absence from the streets of San Francisco for almost two years, Muni's first car was stripped down to its frame and completely rebuilt in anticipation of the centennial of the San Francisco Municipal Railway, the nation's first publicly operated major transit system. Returned to the city just before its 98th birthday, car 1 is ready to enter a second century of service to the people of San Francisco. As it marks the beginning of Muni's second century, San Francisco celebrates its municipal railway—an experiment by a "government of better intentions." While at any time one can easily focus on any of many flaws, at this occasion, we celebrate the equation for Muni's success: a bold vision, political will, sound planning, skillful engineering, competent management, high service level, safe operation, good maintenance, and dedicated workers. (SFMR Y20110414.)

This book has been a collaborative effort by a group of authors who have a lifelong appreciation of the achievements of the San Francisco Municipal Railway. The authors' royalties of this book have been donated to Muni's not-for-profit partner, the Market Street Railway, to further the programs of its San Francisco Railway Museum. The Market Street Railway supports San Francisco's commitment to its transit heritage and sees the historic cars of the F line as "Museums in Motion." Located at 77 Steuart Street just south of Justin Herman Plaza on San Francisco's Embarcadero, the San Francisco Railway Museum is open Tuesday through Sunday 10:00 a.m. to 6:00 p.m. Visit MSR's website, www.streetcar.org, to learn more about San Francisco transit history, the Market Street Railway's partnership with Muni, and its various volunteer opportunities to help sustain San Francisco as America's best streetcar city. (Courtesy Peter Ehrlich.)

www.arcadiapublishing.com

Discover books about the town where you grew up, the cities where your friends and families live, the town where your parents met, or even that retirement spot you've been dreaming about. Our Web site provides history lovers with exclusive deals, advanced notification about new titles, e-mail alerts of author events, and much more.

MADE IN THE USA

Arcadia Publishing, the leading local history publisher in the United States, is committed to making history accessible and meaningful through publishing books that celebrate and preserve the heritage of America's people and places. Consistent with our mission to preserve history on a local level, this book was printed in South Carolina on American-made paper and manufactured entirely in the United States.

This book carries the accredited Forest Stewardship Council (FSC) label and is printed on 100 percent FSC-certified paper. Products carrying the FSC label are independently certified to assure consumers that they come from forests that are managed to meet the social, economic, and ecological needs of present and future generations.

FSC
Mixed Sources
Product group from well-managed
forests and other controlled sources

Cert no. SW-COC-001530
www.fsc.org
© 1996 Forest Stewardship Council

Find Your Place in History.